Small Group Members Are Saying . . .

Six weeks ago we were strangers. Today we are a family in Christ. We talk to each other, lean on each other, encourage each other, and hold each other accountable. We have gone from meeting as a Bible study to getting together for several social events, meeting for Sunday services, and organizing service projects in our community.

—Sandy and Craig

The Purpose-Driven material quickly moved us beyond group and closer toward family, beyond reading God's Word to knowing God!

—The Coopers

Small Group Leaders Are Saying . . .

Even though our group has been together for several years, the questions in this study have allowed us to connect on a much deeper level. Many of the men are displaying emotions we haven't seen before.

—Steve and Jennifer

The material has become a personal compass to me. When I find myself needing to make a decision, I ask, "Does it bring me closer to God's family? Does it make me more like Christ? Am I using the gifts God gave me? Am I sharing God's love? Am I surrendering my life to please God?" I still have a long way to go, but this has been a blessing and a compass to keep me on his path.

—Craig

Pastors and Church Leaders Are Saying . . .

We took the entire church through this curriculum, and the results were nothing less than miraculous. Our congregation was ignited with passion for God and his purposes for our lives. It warmed up the entire congregation as we grew closer to God by "Doing Life Together."

—Kerry

The Purpose-Driven format helped our groups realize there are some areas that they are doing very well in (fellowship and discipleship) and other areas that they need to do some work in. What is amazing is to see how they are committing to work on these areas (especially evangelism and ministry).

—Steve

Other Studies in the DOING LIFE TOGETHER Series

After you complete this study, we'd love to hear how DOING LIFE TOGETHER has affected your life, your group, or your church! Write us at stories@lifetogether.com. You can also log on to www.lifetogether.com to see how others are putting "life together" into practice.

BEGINNING
LIFE TOGETHER

six sessions on
God's purposes
for your life

written by
BRETT and **DEE EASTMAN**
TODD and **DENISE WENDORFF**
KAREN LEE-THORP

GRAND RAPIDS, MICHIGAN 49530 USA

ZONDERVAN™

Beginning Life Together
Copyright © 2002 by Brett and Deanna Eastman, Todd and Denise Wendorff, and Karen Lee-Thorp

Requests for information should be addressed to:

Zondervan, *Grand Rapids, Michigan 49530*

ISBN 0-310-24672-5

Interior icons by Tom Clark

Printed in the United States of America

03 04 05 06 07 08 /❖ DC/ 10 9

CONTENTS

FOREWORD

Over twenty-five years ago I noticed a little phrase in Acts 13:36 that forever altered the direction of my life. It read, *"David had served God's purpose in his own generation."* I was fascinated by that simple yet profound summary of David's life, and I determined to make it the goal of my life, too. I would seek to discover and fulfill the purposes for which God had created me.

This decision provoked a number of questions: What are God's purposes for putting us on earth? What does a purpose-driven life look like? How can the church enable people to fulfill God's eternal purposes? I read through the Bible again and again, searching for the answers to these questions. As a direct result of what I learned, my wife, Kay, and I decided to start Saddleback Church and build it from the ground up on God's five purposes for us (which are found in the New Testament).

In the living laboratory of Saddleback Church, we were able to experiment with different ways to help people understand, apply, and live out the purposes of God. I've written two books about the lessons we've learned (*The Purpose-Driven Church* and, more recently, *The Purpose-Driven Life*). As other churches became interested in what we were doing, we began sharing the tools, programs, and studies we developed at Saddleback. Over a million copies of *The Purpose-Driven Church* are now in print in some nineteen languages, and The Purpose-Driven Class Curriculum (Class 101–401) is now used in tens of thousands of churches around the world. We hope that the same will be true for this exciting new small group curriculum.

DOING LIFE TOGETHER is a groundbreaking study in several ways. It is the first small group curriculum built completely on the purpose-driven paradigm. This is not just another study to be used *in* your church; it is a study *on* the church to help *strengthen* your church. Many small group curricula today are quite self-focused and individualistic. They generally do not address the importance of the local church and our role in it as believers. Another unique feature of this curriculum is its balance. In every session, the five purposes of God are stressed in some way.

But the greatest reason I am excited about releasing this DOING LIFE TOGETHER curriculum is that I've seen the dramatic changes it produces in the lives of those who study it. These small group studies were not developed in some detached ivory tower or academic setting but in the day-to-day ministry of Saddleback Church, where thousands of people meet weekly in small groups that are committed to fulfilling God's purposes. This curriculum has been tested and retested, and the results have been absolutely amazing. Lives have been changed, marriages saved, and families strengthened. And our church has grown—in the past seven years we've seen over 9,100 new believers baptized at Saddleback. I attribute these results to the fact that so many of our members are serious about living healthy, balanced, purpose-driven lives.

It is with great joy and expectation that I introduce this resource to you. I am so proud of our development team on this project: Brett and Dee Eastman, Todd and Denise Wendorff, and Karen Lee-Thorp. They have committed hundreds of hours to write, teach, develop, and refine these lessons —with much feedback along the way. This has been a labor of love, as they have shared our dream of helping you serve God's purpose in your own generation. The church will be enriched for eternity as a result.

Get ready for a life-changing journey. God bless!

—Pastor Rick Warren

Pastor Rick Warren is the author of *The Purpose-Driven Church* and *The Purpose-Driven Life* [www.purposedrivenlife.com].

ACKNOWLEDGMENTS

Sometimes in life God gives you a dream. Most of the time it remains only a dream. But every once in a while, a dream captures your heart, consumes your thoughts, and compels you to action. However, if others around you aren't motivated to share the dream and aren't moved to action along with you, it remains just that—a dream. By the grace of God and a clear call on the hearts of a few, our dream has become a reality.

The DOING LIFE TOGETHER series was birthed one summer in the hearts of Brett and Dee Eastman and Todd and Denise Wendorff, two Saddleback Church staff couples. They hoped to launch a new one-year Bible study based on the Purpose-Driven® life. They called it *The Journey: Experiencing the Transformed Life*. *The Journey* was launched with a leadership team that committed its heart and soul to the project. We will never be able to express our gratitude to each of you who shared the dream and helped to continue the dream now, three years later.

Early on, Karen Lee-Thorp, an experienced writer of many Bible studies, joined the team. Oh, God, you are good to us!

Saddleback pastors and staff members too numerous to mention have supported our dream and have come alongside to fan the flames. We would have never gotten this off the ground without their belief and support.

We also want to express our overwhelming gratitude to the numerous ministries and churches that helped shape our spiritual heritage. We're particularly grateful for Bill Bright of Campus Crusade for Christ, who gave us a dream for reaching the world, and for Bill Hybels of Willow Creek Community Church, who gave us a great love and respect for the local church.

Our special thanks goes to Pastor Rick and Kay Warren for sharing the dream of a healthy and balanced purpose-driven church that produces purpose-driven lives over time. It clearly is the basis for the body of this work. God only knows how special you are to us and how blessed we feel to be a part of your team.

Finally, we thank our beloved families who have lived with us, laughed at us, and loved us through it all. We love doing our lives together with you.

DOING LIFE TOGETHER

DOING LIFE TOGETHER is unique in that it was designed in community for community. Four of us have been doing life together, in one way or another, for over fifteen years. We have been in a small group together, done ministry together, and been deeply involved in each other's lives. We have shared singleness, marriage, childbirth, family loss, physical ailments, teenage years, job loss, and, yes, even marital problems.

Our community has not been perfect, but it has been real. We have made each other laugh beyond belief, cry to the point of exhaustion, feel as grateful as one can imagine, and get so mad we couldn't see straight. We've said things we will always regret and shared moments we will never forget, but through it all we have discovered a diamond in the rough—a community that increasingly reflects the character of Jesus Christ. God has used our relationships with each other to deepen our understanding of and intimacy with him. We have come to believe that we cannot fully experience the breadth and depth of the purpose-driven life outside of loving relationships in the family of God (Ephesians 2:19–22; 4:11–13).

Doing life together was God's plan from the beginning of time. From the relationships of Father, Son, and Holy Spirit in the Trinity, to the twelve apostles, to the early house churches, and even Jesus' final words in the Great Commission (Matthew 28:16–20)—all share the pattern of life together. God longs to connect all of his children in loving relationships that cultivate the five biblical purposes of the church deep within their hearts. With this goal in mind, we have created the DOING LIFE TOGETHER series—the first purpose-driven small group series.

The series is designed to walk you and your group down a path, six weeks at a time over the course of a year, to help you do the purpose-driven life together. There are six study guides in this series. You can study them individually, or you can follow the one-year path through the six studies. *Beginning Life Together* offers a six-week overview of the purpose-driven life. The other five guides (*Connecting with God's Family, Growing to Be Like Christ, Developing Your SHAPE to Serve Others, Sharing Your Life Mission Every Day,* and *Surrendering Your Life for God's Pleasure*) each explore one of the five purposes of the church more deeply.

In his book *The Purpose-Driven Life*, Rick Warren invites you to commit to live a purpose-driven life every day. The DOING LIFE TOGETHER series was designed to help you live this purpose-driven life through being part of a purpose-driven small group. A purpose-driven group doesn't simply connect people in community or grow people through Bible study. These groups seek to help each member balance all five biblical purposes of the church. The five-fold purpose of a healthy group parallels the fivefold purpose of the church.

Beginning Life Together

Beginnings in life are usually big events. They represent things that are new, a first, exciting, scary, and usually faith producing. The five of us know what it's like to join a new small group: "Am I going to fit in here? Is the group worth my time?" When Todd first joined a group, he didn't like all the touchy-feely "sharing." Karen showed up at her first group only because she was interested in a guy. Brett wasn't even sure he wanted to be a Christian. Dee felt shy around so many unfamiliar faces, but Denise's top concern was, "Will it be fun?" Perhaps we're not so different from Jesus' first disciples, who joined his group with widely different backgrounds and expectations. Jesus accepted them as they were, but challenged them to become something more.

You may be getting involved in your first group—or perhaps you're using this study guide with a group you've known for years. Either way, *Beginning Life Together* will get you going on a whole new adventure. This guide will provide an overview of the timeless pathway God created to fulfill his plan for your life. It will help you not only understand but experience the five biblical purposes that he intended for every one of his children.

The first words of the Bible are "in the beginning God created...." And after God created everything in heaven and earth, he blessed his creation and said that it was "very good." May you experience God's full blessing as you begin this new series. Finally, know in your heart that, as with the beginning of life itself, your beginning of *life together* is very good in his eyes.

Outline of Each Session

Most people desire to live a purpose-driven life, but few people actually achieve this on a consistent basis. That's why we've included elements of all five purposes in every meeting—so that you can live a healthy, balanced spiritual life over time.

When you see the following symbols in this book, you will know that the questions and exercises in that section promote that particular purpose.

CONNECTING WITH GOD'S FAMILY (FELLOWSHIP). The foundation for spiritual growth is an intimate connection with God and his family. The questions in this section will help you get to know the members of your small group so that you'll begin to feel a sense of belonging. This section is designed to open your time together and provide a fun way to share your personal stories with one another.

GROWING TO BE LIKE CHRIST (DISCIPLESHIP). This is the most exciting portion of each lesson. Each week you'll study one or two core passages from the Bible. The focus will be on how the truths from God's Word make a difference in your lives. We will often provide an experiential exercise to enable you not just to talk about the truth but also to experience it in a practical way.

DEVELOPING YOUR SHAPE TO SERVE OTHERS (MINISTRY). Most people want to know how God has uniquely shaped them for ministry and where they can serve in the center of his will. This section will help make that desire a reality. Every other week or so you will be encouraged to take practical steps in developing who God uniquely made you to be in order to serve him and others better.

SHARING YOUR LIFE MISSION EVERY DAY (EVANGELISM). Many people skip over this aspect of the Christian life because it's scary, relationally awkward, or simply too much work for their busy schedules. We understand, because we have these thoughts as well. But God calls all of us to reach out a hand to people who don't know him. It's much easier to take practical, manageable steps that can be integrated naturally into everyday life if you take them together. Every other week or so you will have an opportunity to take a small step.

SURRENDERING YOUR LIFE FOR GOD'S PLEASURE (WORSHIP). A surrendered heart is what pleases God most. Each small group session will give you a chance to surrender your heart to God and one another in prayer. In addition, you'll be introduced to several forms of small group worship, including listening to worship CDs, singing together, reading psalms, and participating in Communion. This portion of your meeting will transform your life in ways you never thought possible. If you're new to praying in a small group, you won't be pressed to pray aloud until you feel ready.

STUDY NOTES. This section provides background notes on the Bible passage(s) you examine in the GROWING section. You may want to refer to these notes during your study.

FOR FURTHER STUDY. This section can help your more spiritually mature members take the session one step further each week on their own. If your group is ready for deeper study or is comfortable doing homework, this section and the following two sections will help you get there. You may want to encourage them to read these passages and reflect on them in a personal journal or in the Notes section at the end of each session.

PURPOSE-DRIVEN LIFE READING PLAN. This plan for reading *The Purpose-Driven Life* by Rick Warren parallels the weekly sessions in this study guide. *The Purpose-Driven Life* is the perfect complement to the DOING LIFE TOGETHER series. If your group hasn't read the book (or wants to further understand and apply the material taught in the book), you can simply read the recommended selections each week, write a reflection, and discuss the teaching as a group or in pairs. See page 73 for a comprehensive list of the entire forty-day reading plan.

DAILY DEVOTIONS. One of the easiest ways for your group to grow together is to encourage each other to read God's Word on a regular basis. It's so much easier to stay motivated in this area if you have one another's support. On page 72 is a daily reading plan that parallels the study and helps you deepen your walk with God. There are five readings per week. If you really want to grow, we suggest you pair up with a friend (spiritual partner) to encourage each other throughout the week. Decide right now, and write the name of someone you'd like to join with for the next six weeks.

THE GOAL OF LIFE

By the time I finished college, I knew I wanted to live my life for Jesus Christ and nothing else. Nothing could compare to knowing and loving him. Todd had made the same commitment. This shared commitment seemed like the foundation for a happy marriage, so we took the plunge. It wasn't long, though, before reality rolled in like a tidal wave. We were mad at each other all the time! He had his way of doing things, and I had mine. Everything was a power struggle. We both loved Jesus and were even serving him full-time as our vocation. But there was one thing we'd overlooked: we had no idea how to love one another. We had built our house on a solid foundation, but the walls were flimsy and the roof was sagging.

Once this began to dawn on us, we set about learning to love. Day after day, year after year, we struggled but pressed on. We learned to put our own agendas aside, to believe in each other, to see each other as more important than ourselves. As I looked with new eyes at the extent of God's love for me, this understanding slowly transformed my heart toward Todd. Our marriage is still a work in progress, but God is teaching us how to build a house of love.

Learning to love has been a theme in all our relationships—with friends, coworkers, and even strangers. It's often easier to love God privately than to love the flawed people around us. But at the heart of God's purposes for us is his longing that we will learn to give and receive love as richly as he does.

—Denise

CONNECTING WITH GOD'S FAMILY   20 min.

Doing Life together begins with simply getting to know one another. A great way to do this is to tell something of your life story. In this session you'll begin on a lighthearted note by playing a game called "Two Truths and a Lie."

1. The leader goes first. Tell the group three things about yourself. Two of these things must be true, and one must be something you've made up. Then each group member gets to guess

which of the three statements is false. After everyone has guessed, the leader reveals which statement was the lie. Each person who guessed right gets one point. The leader gets three points if no one guesses correctly.

Continue around the circle until everyone has told two truths and a lie. Then add up your points and give a round of applause to the winner.

2. It's important for every group to agree on a set of shared values. If your group doesn't already have an agreement (sometimes called a covenant), turn to page 61. Even if you've been together for some time and your values are clear, the Purpose-Driven Group Agreement can help your group achieve greater health and balance. We recommend that you especially consider rotating group leadership, setting up spiritual partners, and introducing purpose teams into the group. Simply go over the values and expectations listed in the agreement to be sure everyone in the group understands and accepts them. Make any necessary decisions about such issues as refreshments and child care.

 GROWING TO BE LIKE CHRIST   30 min.

What's the point of life here on earth? Why does life together even matter? In a few brief sentences, Jesus sketches what's important in life:

> Hearing that Jesus had silenced the Sadducees, the Pharisees got together. ³⁵One of them, an expert in the law, tested him with this question: ³⁶"Teacher, which is the greatest commandment in the Law?"
>
> ³⁷Jesus replied: "'Love the Lord your God with all your heart and with all your soul and with all your mind.' ³⁸This is the first and greatest commandment. ³⁹And the second is like it: 'Love your neighbor as yourself.' ⁴⁰All the Law and the Prophets hang on these two commandments."
>
> —Matthew 22:34–40

3. Jesus says that loving God and loving our neighbors should be our two top life goals. Why do you suppose he chose these two goals instead of others? (For instance, why isn't self-fulfillment on his list? Why doesn't he cite a longer set of rules?)

4. *Love* is an abstract idea. On a practical level, how does a person go about loving God?

5. Share some examples of how people you know have loved a neighbor (family member, coworker, and the like) well. What does love look like in action?

6. Do you think it's possible to love God without loving our neighbors? Explain your reasoning.

7. What do you think happens when someone tries to love others without loving God?

Not long after this incident with the Pharisees, Jesus knew he was about to be arrested and killed. He gave his followers another command to add to the first two:

"A new command I give you: Love one another. As I have loved you, so you must love one another. ³⁵By this all men will know that you are my disciples, if you love one another."

—John 13:34–35

8. How is this new command like the two earlier ones?

How is it different?

9. What's your reaction to the idea that the Christian life boils down to relationships—love for God and love for others?

10. In what situation this week will it be challenging for you to love God or others?

Loving God and others can't really be separated. Life together with God means life together with others, and vice versa. In the next five sessions of this study, you'll learn about five steps along a path toward learning to love God and others well. *Learning to love*—that's the point of life on earth.

SHARING YOUR LIFE MISSION EVERY DAY   10 min.

God is so full of love that he created humans so that he could love and be loved by us. He sent Jesus to draw us into his family of love. Love isn't meant to be hoarded; it's meant to be given away! You've now tasted a loving connection with each other in this group. The beginning of a group is a wonderful time to welcome a few new people into your circle.

11. Do you know anyone who would benefit from a group like this? Who could that person be? Think about family members, friends, neighbors, parents of your kids' friends, church members, coworkers, and the people who share your hobbies. Take a moment now to prayerfully list one or two names, and then share the names with your group.

NAME	NAME

12. Pull an open chair into the circle of your group. This chair represents someone you could invite to join your group. Take a moment to pray together for the people whose names you wrote down.

Commit to

- making the call this week. Why not?—over 50 percent of those invited to a small group say yes! You may even want to invite him or her to ride with you.
- calling your church office to get the names of new members, and inviting new members who live near you to visit your group.
- serving your group by praying for and welcoming new people to your group.

SURRENDERING YOUR LIFE FOR GOD'S PLEASURE 15–30 min.

13. Gather into circles of three or four people so that everyone has time to share and pray. Allow everyone to answer this question: "How can we pray for you this week?" You can write down prayer requests in the Prayer and Praise Report on page 74.

Take some time to pray for these requests. Ask God to empower you with love for the people on your hearts. Anyone who isn't used to praying aloud should feel free to offer prayers in silence. Or, if you're new to prayer and you're feeling brave, try praying just one sentence: "God, please help me to love

_____."

STUDY NOTES

An expert in the Jewish law. The law is the teaching laid down in the first five books of the Bible—the very part of the Bible that Jesus quotes in this passage. The goal of life has been laid down from the beginning and hasn't changed.

Heart . . . soul . . . mind. These words overlapped in Jewish usage. The heart, for example, was regarded as the source of one's deepest beliefs, motives, desires, and feelings. It didn't signify merely the emotions. The point of using all these words was to emphasize the call to love God with *every* part of us— emotions, reasoning, imagination, passion, will, energy, and actions. Loving God is not just an emotion, nor is it just a belief. It also involves our will. We put our soul into it and do something to make love a reality.

Neighbor. The Jews debated who was and wasn't a "neighbor" who deserved love. Jesus expanded the word to include *everyone* who crosses our path (Luke 10:29–37). Today people who live on the other side of the planet are our neighbors, because our lives are linked with theirs.

☐ *For Further Study* on this topic, read *Leviticus 19:9–18;*
Deuteronomy 6:4–5; 10:12–13; Proverbs 4:23; 1 John 3:16–18;
4:7–12, 20–21.

☐ *The Purpose-Driven Life Reading Plan:* Days 1–7

☐ *See page 73 for a checklist of the complete forty-day reading plan.*

NOTES

If you're using the DVD along
with this curriculum, please use
this space to take notes on the
teaching for this session.

CONNECTING WITH GOD'S FAMILY

I was at the lowest point in my Christian life. I had lost my job, felt far away from God, and had slipped into a mild depression. To make matters worse, my wife and I were living outside of our home state—away from family and lifelong friends. It was a recipe for disaster. I was really stuck. I didn't know who to talk to.

A man at work knew of another man who might be able to help me, so I made the appointment and arrived at the restaurant. I was so emotionally cashed, I would have bawled like a baby in this man's arms if it weren't for the fact that we were in public and I didn't want to let on that I was really hurting. This complete stranger was a fine Christian man who happened to have the same profession as my father . He was a dentist. I immediately bonded with him. He was a lifeline to cling to during those dark months. He helped me rebuild my confidence in God and motivated me to learn how to forgive and how to resolve relational conflict. A year later he was killed in an auto accident while on a mission trip in Africa. I grieved his loss while celebrating the gift of his life. I couldn't have made it through those days without him.

—Todd

CONNECTING WITH GOD'S FAMILY   10 min.

1. One way to strengthen your connection with each other is to tell stories about your connection with God. Please share one of the following.

   • When was the first time you became aware of God's love?
   • When you were growing up, what did your family believe about God?

GROWING TO BE LIKE CHRIST   20 min.

What does a genuine connection with each other look like? Is it enough to go golfing together, talk football, swap the latest gossip, or exchange news about our kids? Many of us are used to easy, pleasant relationships where we share interests but don't have to offer much of our souls. Yet Jesus said, "Love one another." What does that mean? Here is one Scripture passage that offers clues to what happens when we connect:

> Let us hold unswervingly to the hope we profess, for he who promised is faithful. ²⁴And let us consider how we may spur one another on toward love and good deeds. ²⁵Let us not give up meeting together, as some are in the habit of doing, but let us encourage one another—and all the more as you see the Day approaching.
>
> —Hebrews 10:23–25

2. Hope (verse 23) is fervently wanting something you don't yet have. As Christians, what do we hope for?

How can we help each other hold unswervingly to this hope, even when life is difficult?

3. Give some examples of the kinds of "love and good deeds" you think the writer is talking about in verse 24.

4. If someone wanted to spur you on toward love and good deeds, how would you like them to go about it?

Is there anything you would like them *not* to do?

5. Why is meeting together (verse 25) so important? Why can't we just practice our faith on our own?

6. Recall a time when someone encouraged you. What did the person do?

7. If you wanted to encourage someone in this group, what are some ways you could do so?

DEVELOPING YOUR SHAPE TO SERVE OTHERS   10 min.

Life together is a safe place where you can learn to love and be loved. Love involves faithfully showing up when your group meets, encouraging each other, and motivating each other to do good deeds outside the group. It's so much easier to be rich in hope when you have the support of other Christians. That's why God wants you to be connected.

8. Take a moment on your own to rate how well you're doing in each of the following four areas (1 = just beginning; 3 = getting going; 5 = well developed). You won't have to share your answers with the group.

I am deepening my understanding of and friendship with God in community with others	1 2 3 4 5
I am growing in my ability both to share and to show my love to others	1 2 3 4 5
I am willing to share my real needs for prayer and support from others	1 2 3 4 5
I am resolving conflict constructively and am willing to forgive others	1 2 3 4 5

9. Turn to someone sitting next to you and share with this person one strength you have in the area of connecting with others.

The *Connecting with God's Family* study guide in this DOING LIFE TOGETHER series will help you grow in these four areas. Even if you're a beginner at connecting, God is delighted that you're taking a step forward. Just being a part of this group is a huge step! Life together is lived by grace—with plenty of room to make mistakes and the relief of no pressure to perform.

SURRENDERING YOUR LIFE FOR GOD'S PLEASURE   15–20 min.

10. On page 74 is a prayer and praise sheet. It's a place where you can write each other's requests for prayer. You can also make a note when God answers a prayer. What is one thing you'd like this group to pray about for the rest of this study's sessions?

   Pray for each other's requests. If you're new to group prayer, it's okay to pray silently or to pray by using just one sentence:

"God, please help _____ to _____

_____."

STUDY NOTES

We don't know who wrote the letter to the Hebrews, but it must have been a Jewish believer in Christ with high standing in the community, such as Paul, Apollos, or Barnabas. The recipients of this letter were also Jewish believers in Christ. They were under pressure to drift away from Christ and back to the Judaism they had grown up with. Allegiance to Christ was putting them under pressure—both from their Jewish friends and from the Roman government. The book of Hebrews was written to encourage them to persist in their faith despite the increasing costs of doing so. Their connections with each other were vital to their ability to withstand their society's pressures. We, too, need one another's support in the face of life's challenges and our society's secular bent. Otherwise, it's all too easy to settle for a bland Christian veneer on a self-focused life.

Spur one another on. From a verb that means "to stimulate, or incite to action." Our connection should motivate one another to do the acts of love, goodness, and justice that set us apart from the world around us. It should cause good to flow out from each of us.

Encourage one another. The Greek for *encourage* comes from a word (*parakaleō*) that means "to call someone to your side." The Holy Spirit is called the *paraklētos* ("Counselor") in John 14:16, because he is called alongside us to help us. In the same way, we come to each other's side and offer comfort or motivation to action. (See 2 Corinthians 2:7.) Sometimes people need a hug or a listening ear, and sometimes they need to be gently prodded to do something.

☐ **For Further Study** *on this topic, read Hebrews 13:1–5; Titus 3:8–11; 2 Peter 3:10–12; 1 Peter 1:22–2:1; Acts 2:42–47; Matthew 18:20; 1 Thessalonians 5:14–15.*

☐ **The Purpose-Driven Life Reading Plan:** Days 15–21

If you're using the DVD along
with this curriculum, please use
this space to take notes on the
teaching for this session.

GROWING TO BE LIKE CHRIST

When Dee, Denise, and I went to Israel some years ago, we visited a local family's vineyard. It was amazing to stand there and think about Jesus' words about vineyards in the Gospels. Our guide pointed out the rocks holding up the branches of the grapevines. There were big rocks and little rocks, chosen according to the size that would support each branch. He explained that as the vinedresser walks through his vineyard, he not only clips branches that are unproductive but also lifts the productive branches off the ground so they can produce more. He props a rock under each branch that is heavy with grapes, so it can produce freely without breaking under the weight of the grapes.

As our group sat on that hillside, we talked about how we are like those branches. In order to be spiritually fruitful, we need to do whatever it takes to stay connected to Jesus Christ, our true vine. And sometimes we need other people to be like those rocks, holding us up so we don't snap off from the vine in a moment of stress—or even as a result of our fruitfulness.

—Todd

CONNECTING WITH GOD'S FAMILY   10 min.

1. Share an experience that helped you grow spiritually.

GROWING TO BE LIKE CHRIST   30–40 min.

Your life together with God and other Christians begins with *connections*—faith in Jesus, time with Jesus' followers. It grows as you deepen those connections. Jesus uses the image of a grapevine to describe the intimate connection you need for spiritual growth:

> *"I am the Real Vine and my Father is the Farmer. ²He cuts off every branch of me that doesn't bear grapes. And every branch that is grape-bearing he prunes back so it will bear even more. ³You are already pruned back by the message I have spoken.*
>
> *⁴"Live in me. Make your home in me just as I do in you. In the same way that a branch can't bear grapes by itself but only by being joined to the vine, you can't bear fruit unless you are joined with me.*
>
> *⁵"I am the Vine, you are the branches. When you're joined with me and I with you, the relation intimate and organic, the harvest is sure to be abundant. Separated, you can't produce a thing. ⁶Anyone who separates from me is deadwood, gathered up and thrown on the bonfire. ⁷But if you make yourselves at home with me and my words are at home in you, you can be sure that whatever you ask will be listened to and acted upon. ⁸This is how my Father shows who he is—when you produce grapes, when you mature as my disciples.*
>
> —John 15:1–8 THE MESSAGE

2. Picture a vine with many branches. From some of these branches, great bunches of grapes are hanging. What enables the branch to produce grapes?

In what sense does the branch live in, or make its home in, the vine?

3. What can we learn from this image about our connection to Jesus?

4. In practical, day-to-day terms, how does a person go about making a home in Jesus?

5. Even though we are as connected to Jesus as a vine to a branch, what are some of the things that can hinder us from drawing enough nourishment from Jesus?

6. When we make our home in the vine, we bear fruit. What does a fruitful Christian life look like?

7. Some of us try hard to be fruitful but don't put much time into making our home in Jesus. This effort is futile. There's no way to bear real fruit without drawing on the nourishment of an intimate connection with Jesus Christ. Below are just a few of the signs of a fruitful person. Take a moment to evaluate your own fruitfulness (1 = just beginning; 3 = getting going; 5 = well developed). You won't have to share your responses with the group.

I have a growing relationship with God through regular time in the Bible and in prayer (spiritual habits)	1 2 3 4 5
I am experiencing more of the characteristics of Jesus Christ (love, patience, gentleness, courage, self-control, and so forth) in my life	1 2 3 4 5
I am avoiding addictive behaviors (food, television, busyness, and the like) to meet my needs	1 2 3 4 5
I am spending time with a Christian friend (spiritual partner) who celebrates and challenges my spiritual growth	1 2 3 4 5

8. Suppose someone feels bad that he's not as fruitful as he'd like to be. What do you think Jesus would like to say to this person, heart to heart?

9. One key to drawing nourishment from Jesus is simply *time*. You need to devote some time on a regular basis to focus your mind on him. On page 72 you'll find a list of brief Bible passages for daily devotions—five per week (for this week and the next three weeks of this study). If you've never spent daily time with Jesus, this is an easy way to start. You can simply read the passage and pray your thoughts about it to Jesus. Would you be willing to set aside just ten minutes a day for life together with Jesus during the next four weeks? (If you're already spending personal time with God, consider adding an element to deepen your relationship, such as memorizing a verse each week or writing your prayers in a journal. See page 103 for a sample journal page that you can use as a guide.)

 SURRENDERING YOUR LIFE FOR GOD'S PLEASURE 15–30 min.

10. How can the group pray for you this week? (Remember the requests you recorded on your prayer and praise sheet.)

11. As you begin your prayer time, invite one group member to read aloud these words of Jesus while the others shut their eyes and sit in silence: "Live in me. Make your home in me just as I do in you" (John 15:4).

    Then take two minutes of silence to reflect on Jesus' words to you. Allow yourself to hear him saying this to you. Quietly repeat his words. What is Jesus saying to you personally?

After two minutes of silence, you can begin praying aloud.

STUDY NOTES

I am the Real Vine. A branch produces grapes only when it is properly attached to the vine. Grapes were a sign of fruitfulness in the lives of God's people, both in the Old and New Testaments. (See Isaiah 5:1–7, for example.)

Cuts off. Jesus is drawing a distinction between those who have faith in him (those who make their home in him and bear fruit) and those who don't. Faithless branches, like Judas, will be cut off. If you love Jesus and desire to follow him, you don't have to live in fear of being cut off. Instead, you can expect to be pruned.

Prunes. "New plants are pruned for three to five years to 'train' them before they are allowed to produce a crop."* The word *kathaireō* means "to purify," or "to cleanse." Removing dead wood brings new life back to the branch. Pruning may be the process by which sin (a bad habit or an attitude) is removed from our lives to make us more fruitful.

Live in me. Some other translations read, "Abide [or remain, *menō*] in me." To abide is "to remain, to dwell, to endure." In John 15:10, Jesus links remaining in him with obeying him: "If you obey my commands, you will remain in my love, just as I have obeyed my Father's commands and remain in his love." In 1 John 2:24, John links remaining in Jesus with faithfulness to the gospel: "See that what you have heard from the beginning remains in you. If it does, you also will remain in the Son and in the Father." True belief and consistent behavior can't be separated—people who truly believe will consistently do what pleases Jesus. The writers of the New Testament could scarcely imagine our current situation in which many people pray to accept Jesus as their Savior but then don't go on to live as he taught. They assumed that we who are making our home in Jesus would draw nourishment from him so that we would have the strength to obey him. We draw nourishment from the Vine by praying, reading the Bible, filling our minds with thoughts of God, and developing an awareness of God's constant presence (Psalm 16:8).

☐ *For Further Study* on this topic, read Hebrews 12:5–11; 2 John 9; 1 John 2:28; 3:17; Psalm 15.

☐ *The Purpose-Driven Life Reading Plan:* Days 22–28

The Life Application Commentary Series, CD-ROM. Copyright © 1997, 1998, 1999, and 2000 by the Livingstone Corporation. Produced with permission of Tyndale House Publishers. All rights reserved.

NOTES

If you're using the DVD along with this curriculum, please use this space to take notes on the teaching for this session.

DEVELOPING YOUR SHAPE TO SERVE OTHERS

Brett and Todd got to know each other in seminary. Todd joked that Brett was taking seminary by extension—Brett often had to borrow Todd's notes because he was so engrossed in doing ministry that he'd get to class late.

Three years after seminary, Todd and Brett joined the staff of the same church. Along with Dee and Denise, they entered the same small group for couples. One thing the group did, which changed all of their lives, was to give each member extended time to share his or her spiritual story. They heard what each person loved to do and how God had used their life experiences to shape them for particular ways of serving him. After each group member shared, it was natural for others to reflect back their affirmations of how they saw that person contributing uniquely to God's work. The group coached one another on next steps in their relationships with God and in ministry.

Members began to contribute their unique gifts to the group. Todd, for instance, often brought word studies to deepen the group's understanding of a Bible passage. Denise used her gift of hospitality to coordinate the hosting of meetings and the sharing of meals. Brett helped the group deepen connections with one another. Dee came up with ways for group members to experience what they were studying. The group provided a crucial setting for discerning and using the unique ways God had designed them to serve him.

CONNECTING WITH GOD'S FAMILY   10 min.

1. Share one of the following:

   • What is one thing you do that gives you great pleasure?
   • What is one thing you are good at doing?

GROWING TO BE LIKE CHRIST   30–40 min.

Serving God by doing something he wants done is a way of expressing your love for him. Serving another person by meeting a need in his or her life is likewise an expression of love. As you begin to serve one another and serve outsiders together, your small group will acquire a deeper richness than you could have by being involved only in Bible study and prayer.

Maybe you don't think you have much to offer as a servant of God. But he has entrusted you with gifts, abilities, and passions that no other person can match. Jesus told a story to explain how servanthood works in his kingdom. Like most of his stories, this one uses shock value and a sense of humor to make a point:

> "Again, [God's kingdom] will be like a man going on a journey, who called his servants and entrusted his property to them. ¹⁵To the one he gave five talents of money, to another two talents, and to another one talent, each according to his ability. Then he went on his journey. ¹⁶The man who had received the five talents went at once and put his money to work and gained five more. ¹⁷So also, the one with the two talents gained two more. ¹⁸But the man who had received the one talent went off, dug a hole in the ground and hid his master's money.
>
> ¹⁹"After a long time the master of those servants returned and settled accounts with them. ²⁰The man who had received the five talents brought the other five. 'Master,' he said, 'you entrusted me with five talents. See, I have gained five more.'
>
> ²¹"His master replied, 'Well done, good and faithful servant! You have been faithful with a few things; I will put you in charge of many things. Come and share your master's happiness!'
>
> ²²"The man with the two talents also came. 'Master,' he said, 'you entrusted me with two talents; see, I have gained two more.'
>
> ²³"His master replied, 'Well done, good and faithful servant! You have been faithful with a few things; I will put you in charge of many things. Come and share your master's happiness!'
>
> ²⁴"Then the man who had received the one talent came. 'Master,' he said, 'I knew that you are a hard man, harvesting

where you have not sown and gathering where you have not scattered seed. ²⁵So I was afraid and went out and hid your talent in the ground. See, here is what belongs to you.'

²⁶"His master replied, 'You wicked, lazy servant! So you knew that I harvest where I have not sown and gather where I have not scattered seed? ²⁷Well then, you should have put my money on deposit with the bankers, so that when I returned I would have received it back with interest.

²⁸"'Take the talent from him and give it to the one who has the ten talents. ²⁹For everyone who has will be given more, and he will have an abundance. Whoever does not have, even what he has will be taken from him.'"

—Matthew 25:14–29

2. This story sets up a contrast between the first two servants and the third. They handled the master's "talents" (amounts of money) differently. How did their behavior differ?

3. The servants handled the money differently because they saw their master differently. What did the third servant believe about his master (verses 24–25)?

What do you think the first two servants believed about their master?

4. Another difference may have been the way they viewed themselves. Put yourself in their shoes. What view of yourself would motivate you to take risks to invest your master's money?

What view of yourself would motivate you to hide your master's money in the ground?

5. In what ways are you like the first two servants? In what ways are you like the third servant?

6. The master entrusted "talents" (amounts of money) to his servants. What are some resources that God has entrusted to you?

7. God has entrusted you with a portion of his resources in order to do his work on earth. Investing these resources takes time, effort, courage, trust in God, and many other qualities. What are the main challenges you face as you think about using the resources God has entrusted to you?

8. *(Optional)* Describe a time in your life when you were able to use a resource that God has given you.

 DEVELOPING YOUR SHAPE TO SERVE OTHERS   15–20 min.

9. Right here in this group you can start using the resources God has given you. How can each of you best contribute to your group? It's sometimes hard for a person to see what he or she has to offer; it's easier to see others' strengths. So pool your thoughts. For each group member, discuss together what you think this person would be good at. Below are some areas of service to spark your thinking. Who in your group has a heart for prayer? Who has a flair for social events and celebrations? Who is good at organization and details? Who has a heart for outsiders? (See the suggestions on page 42.)

As the group discusses each member's strengths, it's up to that member to agree (or not) to take on an area of service. Place a check mark next to any area(s) you agree to take on.

- [ ] Plan (or help to plan) a celebration for the end of this study. **(CONNECTING)**
- [ ] Provide refreshments for your group for the rest of this study. **(CONNECTING)**
- [ ] Share something next week with the group about what you've learned from your personal Bible reading. **(GROWING)**
- [ ] Lead the Bible study portion of your next meeting—or the whole meeting. **(GROWING)**
- [ ] Research a question from the group about a Bible passage, and bring back the results. **(GROWING)**
- [ ] Coordinate a simple service project you can do as a group. **(DEVELOPING)**
- [ ] Help the group make an ongoing plan for child care during meetings. **(DEVELOPING)**
- [ ] Invite someone new to join your group when you finish session 6 of this study. **(SHARING)**
- [ ] Lead the opening or closing prayer time in your next meeting. **(SURRENDERING)**
- [ ] Bring to your next meeting a CD with a worship song that is meaningful to you. Play the song at the beginning of your meeting. **(SURRENDERING)**
- [ ] Plan a time of worship to end session 6, perhaps with music from a CD, group singing, reading psalms, or other ideas. **(SURRENDERING)**
- [ ] Other ideas:

 SURRENDERING YOUR LIFE FOR GOD'S PLEASURE   15 min.

10. How can the group pray for you this week? If people agreed to take on areas of service, be sure to pray for them in those areas.

STUDY NOTES

Talent. A talent was a measure of weight, such as a pound or a kilo. Here it refers to a sum of money—a quantity of gold or silver. It has been estimated that a talent was worth six thousand denarii, or about twenty years of work for the average day laborer. A talent was a lot of money. Ten talents was *massive* wealth. We often underestimate the value of the assets God has given us.

To the one he gave. God gives assets to each of us as he sees fit. Some have more of this or that. We're not supposed to compare our assets with another person's but to use to the best of our ability the ones we have.

Put his money to work. The word *ergazomai* means "to labor," or "to minister." In context here, it means to invest.

I will put you in charge of many things. The servant's reward for good service is more opportunities to serve. Some of us might prefer not to be in charge of anything, but God wants more for us than that.

☐ *For Further Study* on this topic, read 1 Peter 4:10; 1 Corinthians 12:1–31; 14:26.

☐ *The Purpose-Driven Life Reading Plan:* Days 29–35

NOTES

If you're using the DVD along with this curriculum, please use this space to take notes on the teaching for this session.

SHARING YOUR LIFE MISSION EVERY DAY

There are numerous Christians today who owe their faith, at least in part, to the writings of the Oxford professor C. S. Lewis. But throughout his teens and twenties, Lewis himself was a committed atheist. What led him to change his ways?

No single person persuaded Lewis to trust Jesus Christ. Rather, it was the combined influence of many people through books, music, and personal encounters that made the difference. In *Surprised by Joy*, Lewis described the effect of simply encountering sane, responsible adults who "believed in a world behind, or around, the material world." He enjoyed G. K. Chesterton's intelligence and sense of humor—despite Chesterton's Christian faith. He was both alarmed and fascinated when he met men who were much like himself but who were actually "attempting strict veracity, chastity, or devotion to duty."* Lewis himself was neither honest nor sexually pure, but he found himself respecting men who were committed to these traits without being passionless prudes. In Lewis's case, the character of ordinary people proved more effective than hearing countless sermons.

CONNECTING WITH GOD'S FAMILY   10 min.

1. Finish this sentence: "When people look at my life, I hope they see someone who ..."

---

*C. S. Lewis, *Surprised by Joy* (New York: Harcourt, Brace & Co., 1955), 175, 192.

GROWING TO BE LIKE CHRIST   30 min.

Francis of Assisi is reported to have said, "Preach the gospel at all times. When necessary, use words." Francis was not minimizing the need to speak about Jesus Christ. He was emphasizing that talk without action is unconvincing. We need to be living demonstrations that the gospel is true. Jesus made this point by comparing us to light in a dark world:

> *"You are the light of the world. A city on a hill cannot be hidden. ¹⁵Neither do people light a lamp and put it under a bowl. Instead they put it on its stand, and it gives light to everyone in the house. ¹⁶In the same way, let your light shine before men, that they may see your good deeds and praise your Father in heaven."*
>
> —Matthew 5:14–16

2. What does it mean to be "the light of the world"?

3. What sorts of "good deeds" do you think will cause unbelievers to become curious about God?

4. Why do you think unbelievers are watching our actions so closely?

5. What helps you be the light of the world?

6. What aspects of life cause your light to lose its radiance?

7. *You* in this passage is plural. You aren't meant to be light by yourself. People are far more convinced when they see how a group of Christians cares for each other and for outsiders. How can your family or your small group be the light of the world?

8. What opportunity do you have to be living evidence of God's goodness this week?

SHARING YOUR LIFE MISSION EVERY DAY   15–20 min.

Your group can be light in a dark world. In fact, turning your group's energy outward, as well as inward, will deepen your connections with one another and speed your spiritual growth.

9. Who are the people in your life who need to see the light of Jesus? Think about your extended family, people you know through your children's school or their sports activities, people you know through shared hobbies, your friends, your neighbors, and your coworkers. Write at least one name here.

Share with the group the name you wrote down. Compile all the names into one Top Ten prayer list—the names of the top ten nonbelievers your group will pray for today. (If your group contains fewer than ten members, your list may be shorter.)

Top Ten List

Who in your group could review this list from time to time and keep group members praying for these people?

10. *(Optional)* Imagine you had a party or barbecue and each of you invited one or two people who don't believe in Jesus. What would these people see when they observed your relationships with each other?

SURRENDERING YOUR LIFE FOR GOD'S PLEASURE   15 min.

11. How can the group pray for you this week?

Pray for the people on your Top Ten list. Pray also for one another, including the requests you recorded on your prayer and praise sheet.

STUDY NOTES

A city on a hill. Possibly Tiberias, a city along the coast of the Sea of Galilee. Built by Herod the Great, it was lit up at night by a multitude of lights. You could see the city from any angle along the shores.

Lamp. People used oil lamps in Jesus' day. They were small enough to fit under a bowl, but no one would have lit a lamp and then covered it. The light would have gone out.

Good deeds. Jesus implies that our conduct in daily life should be different from that of nonbelievers. Our acts of kindness, servanthood, courage, and integrity should distinguish us from others in our communities and workplaces. People are watching to see if what we believe really does make a difference in our lives.

☐ *For Further Study* on this topic, read Ephesians 2:10; 5:1–2; 1 Peter 2:12; Acts 4:13.

☐ *The Purpose-Driven Life Reading Plan:* Days 36–40

NOTES

_____

_____

_____

_____

_____

_____

_____

_____

_____

_____

_____

_____

_____

_____

_____

_____

_____

_____

_____

_____

_____

_____

_____

 If you're using the DVD along with this curriculum, please use this space to take notes on the teaching for this session.

SURRENDERING YOUR LIFE FOR GOD'S PLEASURE

Brett and I attended our couple's Bible study and tried to act like our usual selves. Inside we were aching over a family issue. When the time came to share prayer requests, we told the group about the heartache that was going to take us out of town for the weekend. To our astonishment, the group responded, "Let's stop and not do our normal prayer, but just enfold the two of you and pray." As these wonderful people laid hands on us and prayed, I found myself able to open my hands and surrender the situation to God. Feeling his love through these people, I was able to trust that God was present in the situation and able to use it for his purposes.

When the meeting ended, one person after another came to us with encouragement. One woman helped me think through how I was going to continue to surrender the situation when the weekend came to an end and I would still be grieving. She helped me see how I could help Brett and our children surrender it, too. Another woman offered a relevant book, and another gave me a tape that contained a song that had helped her. A fourth person gave us her phone number to call during the weekend. Everyone saw that we would need support to surrender this issue—not just once but for the long haul. No one tried to fix the situation or correct our feelings; they just let us know that we weren't alone.

—Dee

CONNECTING WITH GOD'S FAMILY   10 min.

1. What comes to mind when you think of the word *surrender*?

GROWING TO BE LIKE CHRIST   30 min.

Life together with God and his family ultimately leads us to surrender ourselves wholly to God. Surrender means trust. It means laying down our defenses and whatever we're using to stay in control. It means entrusting our lives to his loving care. The more we know God, the more willing we are to follow him wherever he leads. Worship is linked to surrender, as we see in Jesus' encounter with a man and a woman:

> Now one of the Pharisees invited Jesus to have dinner with him, so he went to the Pharisee's house and reclined at the table. 37When a woman who had lived a sinful life in that town learned that Jesus was eating at the Pharisee's house, she brought an alabaster jar of perfume, 38and as she stood behind him at his feet weeping, she began to wet his feet with her tears. Then she wiped them with her hair, kissed them and poured perfume on them.
>
> 39When the Pharisee who had invited him saw this, he said to himself, "If this man were a prophet, he would know who is touching him and what kind of woman she is—that she is a sinner."
>
> 40Jesus answered him, "Simon, I have something to tell you."
>
> "Tell me, teacher," he said.
>
> 41"Two men owed money to a certain moneylender. One owed him five hundred denarii, and the other fifty. 42Neither of them had the money to pay him back, so he canceled the debts of both. Now which of them will love him more?"
>
> 43Simon replied, "I suppose the one who had the bigger debt canceled."
>
> "You have judged correctly," Jesus said.
>
> 44Then he turned toward the woman and said to Simon, "Do you see this woman? I came into your house. You did not give me any water for my feet, but she wet my feet with her tears and wiped them with her hair. 45You did not give me a kiss, but this woman, from the time I entered, has not stopped kissing my feet. 46You did not put oil on my head, but she has poured perfume on my feet. 47Therefore, I tell you, her many sins have been forgiven—for she loved much. But he who has been forgiven little loves little."

48Then Jesus said to her, "Your sins are forgiven."

49The other guests began to say among themselves, "Who is this who even forgives sins?"

50Jesus said to the woman, "Your faith has saved you; go in peace."

—Luke 7:36–50

2. Look at how the woman in this story expresses her love for Jesus (verses 37–38). In what ways does her behavior resemble worship?

3. Why does Simon the Pharisee view this scene with contempt?

4. What is the point of the story Jesus tells in verses 41–42?

5. The difference between the woman and Simon is that she knows she needs a lot of forgiveness, and he doesn't. On a typical weekday in your life, to what degree are you like either the woman or Simon?

6. Today we don't have Jesus' literal feet available to kiss, so we have to express our worship in others ways. How can we express the kind of love for Jesus that this woman expressed?

7. Out of love for Jesus, this woman surrenders a valuable possession (the jar of perfume) and exposes herself to ridicule. She is a picture of humble surrender. What will it look like for you to surrender your life to Jesus this week?

DEVELOPING YOUR SHAPE TO SERVE OTHERS   15 min.

8. What's next for your group? Turn to the Purpose-Driven Group Agreement on page 61. Do you want to agree to continue meeting together? If so, do you want to change anything in this agreement (times, dates, shared values, and so on)? Are there any things you'd like the group to do better as it moves forward? What will you study—perhaps another book in this series? Take notes on this discussion.

Whether your group is continuing or ending, take a moment to thank your leader(s) and host(s).

SURRENDERING YOUR LIFE FOR GOD'S PLEASURE   30 min.

The woman in the Scripture passage (Luke 7) surrendered herself so completely that bystanders thought it was a shocking display. Deeply humble surrender can make us uneasy—unless we're convinced that God deserves this kind of treatment. But when we comprehend the miracle of his forgiveness, surrender seems like the only natural response.

9. Pair up with one other person. If there is an area of your life that you feel led to surrender to God, you can share it with this person. It might be a difficulty you're facing, a habit you'd like to let go of, a hurt you've been holding on to, or something precious that you want to entrust to God. It could be a particular person. (If there's no specific area that you want to talk about, that's fine.)

Then pray a simple prayer of surrender for yourselves and one another. If you like, you can pray part or all of this prayer:

Father, we love you because you have forgiven us for so much. We trust you because you have shown us your faithfulness. We put all our desires, our dreams, our hurts, our need for healing, our loved ones, our past, and our future into your hands. We open ourselves to your instruction. We trust you to do only what will bring our highest good. We will follow wherever you lead. We say this in your Son's name. Amen.

STUDY NOTES

Reclined. As was customary at that time, the guests dined while lying down on their sides, propped up on one elbow. Jesus' feet were thus stretched out beside him.

Alabaster jar of perfume. "Alabaster jars were carved, expensive, and beautiful. Such jars were made from a translucent, compact gypsum, carved with a long neck that was to be broken off when the contents were poured out. This jar held an expensive perfume. Many Jewish women wore a small perfume flask on a cord around their neck. This jar of perfume would have been valued very highly by this woman."*

She wiped [Jesus' feet] with her hair, kissed them and poured perfume on them. The woman intended to wipe the perfume on Jesus' feet, but she had begun to cry. Her tears fell on his feet, so she wiped them with her hair. Her weeping was probably a sign of deep remorse for sin. It was considered scandalous for a woman to unbind her hair in public, and kissing someone's feet was beyond shocking. The whole display had overtones of illicit love.

☐ *For further study* on this topic, read Romans 3:23; 5:8; 6:23; Isaiah 1:18; Psalm 32; James 4:6–10; Ephesians 2:1–5.

☐ *The Purpose-Driven Life Reading Plan:* Days 8–14

If you're using the DVD along
with this curriculum, please use
this space to take notes on the
teaching for this session.

FREQUENTLY ASKED QUESTIONS

Who may attend the group?

Anybody you feel would benefit from it. As you begin, we encourage each attender to invite at least one other friend to join. A good time to join is in the first or second week of a new study. Share the names of your friends with the group members so that they can be praying for you.

How long will this group meet?

It's totally up to the group—once you come to the end of this six-week study. Most groups meet weekly for at least the first six weeks, but every other week can work as well. At the end of this study, each group member may decide if he or she wants to continue on for another six-week study. We encourage you to consider using the next study in this series. The series is designed to take you on a developmental journey to healthy, purpose-driven lives in thirty-six sessions. However, each guide stands on its own and may be taken in any order. You may take a break between studies if you wish.

Who is the leader?

This booklet will walk you through every step for an effective group. In addition, your group may have selected one or more discussion leaders. We strongly recommend that you rotate the job of facilitating your discussions so that everyone's gifts can emerge and develop. You can share other responsibilities as well, such as bringing refreshments or keeping up with those who miss a meeting. There's no reason why one or two people need to do everything; in fact, sharing ownership of the group will help *everyone* grow. Finally, the Bible says that when two or more are gathered in Jesus' name (which you are), he is there in your midst. Ultimately, God is your leader each step of the way.

Where do we find new members for our group?

This can be troubling, especially for new groups that have only a few people or for existing groups that lose a few people along the way. We encourage you to pray with your group and then brainstorm a list of people from work, church, your neighborhood, your children's school, family, the gym, and so forth. Then have each group member invite several of the people on their list. Another good strategy is to ask church leaders to make an announcement or to allow for a bulletin insert.

No matter how you find members, it's vital that you stay on the lookout for new people to join your group. All groups tend to go through some amount of healthy attrition—the result of moves, releasing new leaders, ministry opportunities, and so forth—and if the group gets too small, it could be at risk of shutting down. If you and your group stay open, you'll be amazed at the people God sends your way. The next person just might become a friend for life. You never know!

How do we handle the child care needs in our group?

Very carefully. Seriously, this can be a sensitive issue. We suggest that you empower the group to openly brainstorm solutions. You may try something that works for some and not for others, so you must just keep playing with the dials. One common solution is to meet in the living room or dining room with the adults and to share the cost of a baby-sitter (or two) who can be with the kids in a different part of the house. Another popular option is to use one home for the kids and a second home (close by or a phone call away) for the adults. Finally, you could rotate the responsibility of providing a lesson of some sort for the kids. This last idea can be an incredible blessing to you and the kids. We've done it, and it's worked great! Again, the best approach is to encourage the group to dialogue openly about both the problem and the solution.

PURPOSE-DRIVEN GROUP AGREEMENT

It's a good idea for every group to put words to their shared values, expectations, and commitments. A written agreement will help you avoid unspoken agendas and disappointed expectations. You'll discuss your agreement in session 1, and then you'll revisit it in session 6 to decide whether you want to modify anything as you move forward as a group. (Alternatively, you may agree to end your group in session 6.) Feel free to modify anything that doesn't work for your group.

If the idea of having a written agreement is unfamiliar to your group, we encourage you to give it a try. A clear agreement is invaluable for resolving conflict constructively and for setting your group on a path to health.

We agree to the following values:

Clear Purpose   To grow healthy spiritual lives by building a healthy small group community. In addition, we _____

_____

_____

_____

Group Attendance   To give priority to the group meeting (call if I will be late or absent)

Safe Environment   To help create a safe place where people can be heard and feel loved (please, no quick answers, snap judgments, or simple fixes)

Confidentiality   To keep anything that is shared strictly confidential and within the group

Spiritual Health   To give group members permission to help me live a healthy spiritual life that is pleasing to God (see the health assessment and health plan)

Inviting People	To keep an open chair in our group and share Jesus' dream of finding a shepherd for every sheep by inviting newcomers
Shared Ownership	To remember that every member is a minister and to encourage each attender to share a small group role or serve on one of the purpose teams (page 64)
Rotating Leaders	To encourage someone new to facilitate the group each week and to rotate homes and refreshments as well (see Small Group Calendar)
Spiritual Partners	To pair up with one other group member whom I can support more diligently and help to grow spiritually (my spiritual partner is _____)

We agree to the following expectations:

• Refreshments/Mealtimes _____

• Child care _____

• When we will meet (day of week) _____

• Where we will meet (place) _____

• We will begin at (time)_____ and end at _____

• We will do our best to have some or all of us attend a worship service together. Our primary worship service time will be _____

• Review date of this agreement: _____

We agree to the following commitment:

Father, to the best of my ability, in light of what I know to be true, I commit the next season of my life to CONNECTING with your family, GROWING to be more like Christ, DEVELOPING my shape for ministry, SHARING my life mission every day, and SURRENDERING my life for your pleasure.

_____	_____	_____
Name	Date	Spiritual Partner (witness)

SMALL GROUP
CALENDAR

Healthy purpose-driven groups share responsibilities and group ownership. This usually doesn't happen overnight but progressively over time. Sharing responsibilities and ownership ensures that no one person carries the group alone. The calendar below can help you in this area. You can also add a social event, mission project, birthdays, or days off to your calendar. This should be completed after your first or second meeting. Planning ahead will facilitate better attendance and greater involvement from others.

Date	Lesson	Location	Dessert/Meal	Facilitator
Monday, January 15	1	Steve and Laura's	Joe	Bill

PURPOSE
TEAM ROLES

The Bible makes clear that every member, not just the small group leader, is a minister in the body of Christ. In a purpose-driven small group (just like in a purpose-driven church), every member plays a role on the team. Review the team roles and responsibilities below and have each member volunteer for a role, or have the group suggest a role for each member. It's best to have one or two people on each team, so you have each purpose covered. Serving in even a small capacity will not only help your leader grow but will also make the group more fun for everyone. Don't hold back. Join a team!

The opportunities below are broken down by the five purposes and then by a *crawl* (beginning group role), *walk* (intermediate group role), or *run* (advanced group role). Try to cover the crawl and walk phases if you can.

Purpose Team Roles	Purpose Team Members
Fellowship Team (**CONNECTING** with God's Family)	
Crawl: Host social events or group activities	_____
Walk: Serve as a small group inviter	_____
Run: Lead the CONNECTING time each week	_____
Discipleship Team (**GROWING** to Be Like Christ)	
Crawl: Ensure that each member has a simple plan and a partner for personal devotions	_____
Walk: Disciple a few younger group members	_____
Run: Facilitate the Purpose-Driven Life Health Assessment and Purpose-Driven Life Health Plan processes	_____

Ministry Team (**DEVELOPING** Your Shape for Ministry)

Crawl: Ensure that each member finds a group role _____
or a purpose team responsibility

Walk: Plan a ministry project for the group in the _____
church or community

Run: Help each member discover and develop _____
a SHAPE-based ministry in the church

Evangelism (Missions) Team (**SHARING** Your Life Mission Every Day)

Crawl: Coordinate the group prayer and praise list _____
of non-Christian friends and family members

Walk: Pray for group mission opportunities and _____
plan a group cross-cultural adventure

Run: Plan as a group to attend a holiday service, _____
host a neighborhood party, or create a seeker
event for your non-Christian friends

Worship Team (**SURRENDERING** Your Life for God's Pleasure)

Crawl: Maintain the weekly group prayer and praise _____
list or journal

Walk: Lead a brief worship time in your group _____
(CD/video/a cappella)

Run: Plan a Communion time, prayer walk, foot _____
washing, or an outdoor worship experience

PURPOSE-DRIVEN LIFE HEALTH ASSESSMENT

	Just Beginning	Getting Going	Well Developed

CONNECTING WITH GOD'S FAMILY

I am deepening my understanding of and friendship with God
in community with others — 1 2 3 4 5

I am growing in my ability both to share and to show my love
to others — 1 2 3 4 5

I am willing to share my real needs for prayer and support from
others — 1 2 3 4 5

I am resolving conflict constructively and am willing to forgive
others — 1 2 3 4 5

CONNECTING Total _____

GROWING TO BE LIKE CHRIST

I have a growing relationship with God through regular time in
the Bible and in prayer (spiritual habits) — 1 2 3 4 5

I am experiencing more of the characteristics of Jesus Christ (love,
joy, peace, patience, kindness, self-control, etc.) in my life — 1 2 3 4 5

I am avoiding addictive behaviors (food, television, busyness, and
the like) to meet my needs — 1 2 3 4 5

I am spending time with a Christian friend (spiritual partner) who
celebrates and challenges my spiritual growth — 1 2 3 4 5

GROWING Total _____

DEVELOPING YOUR SHAPE TO SERVE OTHERS

I have discovered and am further developing my unique God-given
shape for ministry — 1 2 3 4 5

I am regularly praying for God to show me opportunities to serve
him and others — 1 2 3 4 5

I am serving in a regular (once a month or more) ministry in the
church or community — 1 2 3 4 5

I am a team player in my small group by sharing some group role
or responsibility — 1 2 3 4 5

DEVELOPING Total _____

SHARING YOUR LIFE MISSION EVERY DAY

I am cultivating relationships with non-Christians and praying
for God to give me natural opportunities to share his love   1 2 3 4 5

I am investing my time in another person or group who needs
to know Christ personally   1 2 3 4 5

I am regularly inviting unchurched or unconnected friends to
my church or small group   1 2 3 4 5

I am praying and learning about where God can use me and
our group cross-culturally for missions   1 2 3 4 5

SHARING Total _____

SURRENDERING YOUR LIFE FOR GOD'S PLEASURE

I am experiencing more of the presence and power of God in
my everyday life   1 2 3 4 5

I am faithfully attending my small group and weekend services
to worship God   1 2 3 4 5

I am seeking to please God by surrendering every area of my life
(health, decisions, finances, relationships, future, etc.) to him   1 2 3 4 5

I am accepting the things I cannot change and becoming
increasingly grateful for the life I've been given   1 2 3 4 5

SURRENDERING Total_____

Total your scores for each purpose, and place them on the chart below. Reassess
your progress at the end of thirty days. Be sure to select your spiritual partner and
the one area in which you'd like to make progress over the next thirty days.

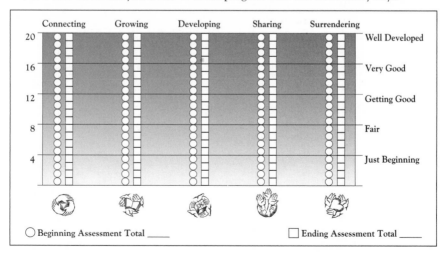

PURPOSE-DRIVEN LIFE HEALTH PLAN

My Name _____ Date _____

My Spiritual Partner _____ Date _____

Possibilities

Plan
(make one goal for each area)

CONNECTING WITH GOD'S FAMILY
Hebrews 10:24–25; Ephesians 2:19
How can I deepen my relationships with others?

- Attend my group more faithfully

- Schedule lunch with a group member

- Begin praying for a spiritual mentor

WHO is/are my shepherd(s)?

NAME: _____

GROWING TO BE LIKE CHRIST
Colossians 1:28; Ephesians 4:15
How can I grow to be like Christ?

- Commit to personal time with God three days a week

- Ask a friend for devotional accountability

- Begin journaling my prayers

WHAT is my Spiritual Health Plan?

RENEWAL DATE: _____

DEVELOPING YOUR SHAPE TO SERVE OTHERS

Ephesians 4:11–13; 1 Corinthians 12:7; 1 Peter 3:10

How can I develop my shape for ministry?

- Begin praying for a personal ministry

- Attend a gift discovery class

- Serve together at a church event or in the community

WHERE am I serving others?

MINISTRY: _____

SHARING YOUR LIFE MISSION EVERY DAY

Matthew 28:18–20; Acts 20:24

How can I share my faith every day?

- Start meeting for lunch with a seeker friend

- Invite a non-Christian relative to church

- Pray for and support an overseas missionary

WHEN am I sharing my life mission?

TIME: _____

SURRENDERING YOUR LIFE FOR GOD'S PLEASURE

How can I surrender my life for God's pleasure?

- Submit one area to God

- Be honest about my struggle and hurt

- Buy a music CD for worship in my car and in the group

HOW am I surrendering my life today?

AREA: _____

	Progress (renew and revise)	Progress (renew and revise)	Progress (renew and revise)
	30 days/Date _____ ☐ ☐ ☐ ☐ Weekly check-in with my spiritual partner or group	60-90 days/Date _____ ☐ ☐ ☐ ☐ Weekly check-in with my spiritual partner or group	120+ days/Date _____ ☐ ☐ ☐ ☐ Weekly check-in with my spiritual partner or group
CONNECTING			
GROWING			
DEVELOPING			
SHARING			
SURRENDERING			

SPIRITUAL PARTNERS'
CHECK-IN PAGE

My Name _____   Spiritual Partner's Name _____

	Our Plans	Our Progress
Week 1		
Week 2		
Week 3		
Week 4		
Week 5		
Week 6		

Briefly check in each week and write down your personal plans and progress for the next week (or even for the next few weeks). This could be done (before or after the meeting) on the phone, through an E-mail message, or even in person from time to time.

DAILY DEVOTIONAL
READINGS

We've experienced so much life change as a result of reading the Bible daily. Hundreds of people have gone through DOING LIFE TOGETHER, and they tell us that the number-one contributor to their growth was the deeper walk with God that came as a result of the daily devotions. We strongly encourage you to have everyone set a realistic goal. Pair people into same-gender spiritual (accountability) partners. This will improve your results tenfold. Then we encourage everyone to take a few minutes each day to **READ** the verse for the day, **REFLECT** on what God is saying to you through the verse, and **RESPOND** to God in prayer in a personal journal. Each of these verses was selected to align with the week's study. After you complete the reading, simply put a check mark in the box next to the verse. Enjoy the journey!

WEEK THREE
- ☐ Luke 6:43–45
- ☐ Luke 6:46–49
- ☐ 1 Peter 2:2–3
- ☐ Psalm 119:165
- ☐ Matthew 5:6

WEEK FOUR
- ☐ Galatians 6:9–10
- ☐ Acts 9:32–42
- ☐ Philippians 2:19–22
- ☐ Exodus 35:20–29
- ☐ Matthew 25:37–40

WEEK FIVE
- ☐ Acts 1:8
- ☐ John 13:35
- ☐ Matthew 13:1–9
- ☐ Matthew 13:18–23
- ☐ Matthew 9:35–38

WEEK SIX
- ☐ Romans 12:1–2
- ☐ 1 Peter 2:4–5
- ☐ Luke 1:26–38
- ☐ Genesis 22:1–18
- ☐ Matthew 5:8

PURPOSE-DRIVEN LIFE READING PLAN

What on Earth Am I Here for?

- ☐ Day 1
- ☐ Day 2
- ☐ Day 3
- ☐ Day 4
- ☐ Day 5
- ☐ Day 6
- ☐ Day 7

Created to Become Like Christ

- ☐ Day 22
- ☐ Day 23
- ☐ Day 24
- ☐ Day 25
- ☐ Day 26
- ☐ Day 27
- ☐ Day 28

Planned for God's Pleasure

- ☐ Day 8
- ☐ Day 9
- ☐ Day 10
- ☐ Day 11
- ☐ Day 12
- ☐ Day 13
- ☐ Day 14

Shaped for Serving God

- ☐ Day 29
- ☐ Day 30
- ☐ Day 31
- ☐ Day 32
- ☐ Day 33
- ☐ Day 34
- ☐ Day 35

Formed for God's Family

- ☐ Day 15
- ☐ Day 16
- ☐ Day 17
- ☐ Day 18
- ☐ Day 19
- ☐ Day 20
- ☐ Day 21

Made for a Mission

- ☐ Day 36
- ☐ Day 37
- ☐ Day 38
- ☐ Day 39
- ☐ Day 40

PRAYER AND
PRAISE REPORT

Briefly share your prayer requests with the large group, making notations below. Then gather in small groups of two, three, or four to pray for each need.

	Prayer Request	Praise Report
Week 1		
Week 2		
Week 3		

	Prayer Request	Praise Report
Week 4		
Week 5		
Week 6		

LEADERSHIP TRAINING

Small Group Leadership 101 (Top Ten Ideas for New Facilitators)

Congratulations! You have responded to the call to help shepherd Jesus' flock. There are few other tasks in the family of God that surpass the contribution you will be making. As you prepare to lead—whether it is one session or the entire series—here are a few thoughts to keep in mind. We encourage you to read these and review them with each new discussion leader before he or she leads.

1. **Remember that you are not alone.** God knows everything about you, and he knew that you would be asked to lead your group. Even though you may not feel ready to lead, this is common for all good leaders. Moses, Solomon, Jeremiah, or Timothy—they *all* were reluctant to lead. God promises, "Never will I leave you; never will I forsake you" (Hebrews 13:5). Whether you are leading for one evening, for several weeks, or for a lifetime, you will be blessed as you serve.

2. **Don't try to do it alone.** Pray right now for God to help you build a healthy leadership team. If you can enlist a coleader to help you lead the group, you will find your experience to be much richer. This is your chance to involve as many people as you can in building a healthy group. All you have to do is call and ask people to help—you'll be surprised at the response.

3. **Just be yourself.** If you won't be you, who will? God wants to use your unique gifts and temperament. Don't try to do things exactly like another leader; do them in a way that fits you! Just admit it when you don't have an answer and apologize when you make a mistake. Your group will love you for it!—and you'll sleep better at night.

4. **Prepare for your meeting ahead of time.** Review the session and the leader's notes, and write down your responses to each question. Pay special attention to exercises that ask group members to do something other than engage in discussion. These exercises will help your group *live* what the Bible teaches, not just talk about it. Be sure you understand how an exercise works, and bring any necessary supplies (such as paper or pens) to your meeting. If the exercise employs one of the items in the appendix (such as the Purpose-Driven Life Health Assessment), be sure to look over that item so

you'll know how it works. Finally, review "Read Me First" on pages 11–14 so you'll remember the purpose of each section in the study.

5. **Pray for your group members by name.** Before you begin your session, go around the room in your mind and pray for each member by name. You may want to review the prayer list at least once a week. Ask God to use your time together to touch the heart of every person uniquely. Expect God to lead you to whomever he wants you to encourage or challenge in a special way. If you listen, God will surely lead!

6. **When you ask a question, be patient.** Someone will eventually respond. Sometimes people need a moment or two of silence to think about the question, and if silence doesn't bother you, it won't bother anyone else. After someone responds, affirm the response with a simple "thanks" or "good job." Then ask, "How about somebody else?" or "Would someone who hasn't shared like to add anything?" Be sensitive to new people or reluctant members who aren't ready to say, pray, or do anything. If you give them a safe setting, they will blossom over time.

7. **Provide transitions between questions.** When guiding the discussion, always read aloud the transitional paragraphs and the questions. Ask the group if anyone would like to read the paragraph or Bible passage. Don't call on anyone, but ask for a volunteer, and then be patient until someone begins. Be sure to thank the person who reads aloud.

8. **Break up into small groups each week, or they won't stay.** If your group has more than seven people, we strongly encourage you to have the group gather in discussion circles of three or four people during the GROW-ING or SURRENDERING sections of the study. With a greater opportunity to talk in a small circle, people will connect more with the study, apply more quickly what they're learning, and ultimately get more out of it. A small circle also encourages a quiet person to participate and tends to minimize the effects of a more vocal or dominant member. And it can help people feel more loved in your group. When you gather again at the end of the section, you can have one person summarize the highlights from each circle.

Small circles are also helpful during prayer time. People who are unaccustomed to praying aloud will feel more comfortable trying it with just two or three others. Also, prayer requests won't take as much time, so circles will have more time to actually pray. When you gather back with the whole group, you can have one person from each circle briefly update everyone on the prayer requests. People are more willing to pray in small circles if they know that the whole group will hear all the prayer requests.

9. **Rotate facilitators weekly.** At the end of each meeting, ask the group who should lead the following week. Let the group help select your weekly facilitator. You may be perfectly capable of leading each time, but you will help others grow in their faith and gifts if you give them opportunities to lead. You can use the Small Group Calendar on page 63 to fill in the names of all six meeting leaders at once if you prefer.

10. **One final challenge (for new or first-time leaders): Before your first opportunity to lead, look up each of the five passages listed below.** Read each one as a devotional exercise to help prepare yourself with a shepherd's heart. Trust us on this one. If you do this, you will be more than ready for your first meeting.

- ☐ Matthew 9:36
- ☐ 1 Peter 5:2-4
- ☐ Psalm 23
- ☐ Ezekiel 34:11–16
- ☐ 1 Thessalonians 2:7–8, 11–12

Small Group Leadership Lifters (Weekly Leadership Tips)

And David shepherded them with integrity of heart;
with skillful hands he led them.

Psalm 78:73

David provides a model of a leader who has a heart for God, a desire to shepherd God's people, and a willingness to develop the skills of a leader. The following is a series of practical tips for new and existing small group leaders. These principles and practices have proved to cultivate healthy, balanced groups in over a thousand examples.

1. Don't Leave Home without It: A Leader's Prayer

"The prayer of a righteous man [or woman] is powerful and effective" (James 5:16). From the very beginning of this study, why not commit to a simple prayer of renewal in your heart and in the hearts of your members? Take a moment right now and write a simple prayer as you begin:

Father, help me _____

_____

_____

2. Pay It Now or Pay It Later: Group Conflict

Most leaders and groups avoid conflict, but healthy groups are willing to do what it takes to learn and grow through conflict. Much group conflict can be avoided if the leader lets the group openly discuss and decide its direction, using the Purpose-Driven Group Agreement. Healthy groups are alive. Conflict is a sign of maturity, not mistakes. Sometimes you may need to get outside counsel, but don't be afraid. See conflict as an opportunity to grow, and always confront it so it doesn't create a cancer that can kill the group over time (Matthew 18:15–20).

3. Lead from Weakness

The apostle Paul said that God's power was made perfect in Paul's weakness (2 Corinthians 12:9). This is clearly the opposite of what most leaders think, but it provides the most significant model of humility, authority, and spiritual power. It was Jesus' way at the cross. So share your struggles along with your successes, confess your sins to one another along with your celebrations, and ask for prayer for yourself along with praying for others. God will be pleased, and your group will grow deeper. If you humble yourself under God's mighty hand, he will exalt you at the proper time (Matthew 23:12).

4. What Makes Jesus Cry: A Leader's Focus

In Matthew 9:35–38, Jesus looked at the crowds following him and saw them as sheep without a shepherd. He was moved with compassion, because they were "distressed and downcast" (NASB); the NIV says they were "harassed and helpless." The Greek text implies that he was moved to the point of tears.

Never forget that you were once one of those sheep yourself. We urge you to keep yourself and your group focused not just inwardly to each other but also outwardly to people beyond your group. Jesus said, "Follow me . . . and I will make you fishers of men" (Matthew 4:19). We assume that you and your group are following him. So how is your fishing going? As leader, you can ignite in your group Jesus' compassion for outsiders. For his sake, keep the fire burning!

5. Prayer Triplets

Prayer triplets can provide a rich blessing to you and many others. At the beginning or end of your group meeting, you can gather people into prayer triplets to share and pray about three non-Christian friends. This single strategy will increase your group's evangelistic effectiveness considerably. Be sure to get an update on the plans and progress from each of the circles. You need only ten minutes at every other meeting—but do this at least once a month. At first, some of your members may feel overwhelmed at the thought of praying for non-Christians. We've been there! But you can be confident that over time they will be renewed in their heart for lost people and experience the blessing of giving birth to triplets.

6. Race against the Clock

When your group grows in size or your members begin to feel more comfortable talking, you will inevitably feel as though you're racing against the clock. You may know the feeling very well. The good news is that there are several simple things that can help your group stick to your agreed schedule:

- The time crunch is actually a sign of relational and spiritual health, so pat yourselves on the back.
- Check in with the group to problem-solve, because they feel the tension as well.

- You could begin your meeting a little early or ask for a later ending time.
- If you split up weekly into circles of three to four people for discussion, you will double the amount of time any one person can share.
- Appoint a timekeeper to keep the group on schedule.
- Remind everyone to give brief answers.
- Be selective in the number of questions you try to discuss.
- Finally, planning the time breaks in your booklet before the group meeting begins can really keep you on track.

7. All for One and One for All: Building a Leadership Team

The statement "Together Everybody Accomplishes More" (TEAM) is especially true in small groups. The Bible clearly teaches that every member is a minister. Be sure to empower the group to share weekly facilitation, as well as other responsibilities, and seek to move every player onto a team over time. Don't wait for people to ask, because it just won't happen. From the outset of your group, try to get everybody involved. The best way to get people in the game is to have the group suggest who would serve best on what team and in what role. See Purpose Team Roles on pages 64–65 for several practical suggestions. You could also talk to people individually or ask for volunteers in the group, but don't miss this opportunity to develop every group member and build a healthy and balanced group over time.

8. Purpose-Driven Groups Produce Purpose-Driven Lives: A Leader's Goal

As you undertake this new curriculum, especially if this is your first time as a leader, make sure you begin with the end in mind. You may have heard the phrase, "If you aim at nothing, you'll hit it every time." It's vital for your group members to review their spiritual health by using the Purpose-Driven Life Health Assessment and Purpose-Driven Life Health Plan (pages 66–70). You'll do part of the health assessment in your group in session 2 and share your results with spiritual partners for support and accountability. Each member will also set one goal for thirty days. The goal will be tied to the purpose you are studying in this particular guide. We strongly encourage you to go even further and do the entire health assessment together. Then during another group session (or on their own), members can set a goal for each of the other four purposes.

Pairing up with spiritual partners will offer invaluable support for that area of personal growth. Encourage partners to pray for one another in the area of their goals. Have partners gather at least three times during the series to share their progress and plans. This will give you and the group the best results. In order for people to follow through with their goals, you'll need to lead with vision and modeling. Share your goals with the group, and update them on how the steps you're taking have been affecting your spiritual life. If you share your progress and plans, others will follow in your footsteps.

9. Discover the Power of Pairs

The best resolutions get swept aside by busyness and forgetfulness, which is why it's important for group members to have support as they pursue a spiritual goal. Have them pair up with spiritual partners in session 2, or encourage them to seek out a Christian coworker or personal mentor. You can promise that they'll never be the same if they simply commit to supporting each other with prayer and encouragement on a weekly basis.

It's best to start with one goal in an area of greatest need. Most of the time the area will be either evangelism or consistent time with the Father in prayer and in Scripture reading. Cultivating time with God is the place to start; if group members are already doing this, they can move on to a second and third area of growth.

You just need a few victories in the beginning. Have spiritual partners check in together at the beginning or end of each group meeting. Ask them to support those check-ins with phone calls, coffee times, and e-mail messages during the week. Trust us on this one—you will see people grow like never before.

10. Don't Lose Heart: A Leader's Vision

You are a strategic player in the heavenly realm. Helping a few others grow in Christ could put you squarely in the sights of Satan himself. First Corinthians 15:58 (NASB) says, "Be steadfast, immovable, always abounding in the work of the Lord." Leading a group is not always going to be easy. Here are the keys to longevity and lasting joy as a leader:

- Be sure to refuel your soul as you give of yourself to others. We recommend that you ask a person to meet with you for personal coaching and encouragement. When asked (over coffee or lunch) to support someone in leadership, nine out of ten people say, "I'd love to!" So why not ask?
- Delegate responsibilities after the first meeting. Doing so will help group members grow, and it will give you a break as well.

- Most important, cultivating your own walk with God puts you on the offensive against Satan and increases the joy zone for everyone in your life. Make a renewed decision right now to make this happen. Don't give Satan a foothold in your heart; there is simply too much at stake.

SESSION ONE:
THE GOAL OF LIFE

Goals of this Session

- To begin to get to know each other
- To discover that love is the point of the Christian life

Especially helpful for this session: Leadership Lifters #1 and #3

Before you meet for the first time, invite as many people as you would enjoy hanging out with. It just makes the group a whole lot more fun for you as the leader. Also, ask one or two people if they'd be willing to colead with you so you don't have to do it alone.

Open your meeting with a brief prayer.

Question 1. This is simply a fun icebreaker. You should be the first to answer this question while others are thinking about how to respond. Appoint someone other than yourself to keep score so that people begin to feel it is *their* group, not just your group.

Be sure to give each person a chance to respond to this question, because it's an opportunity for the group to get to know each other. It's not necessary to go around the circle in order.

Introduction to the Series. If this is your first study guide in the DOING LIFE TOGETHER series, you'll need to take some time after question 1 to orient the group to one principle that undergirds the series: *A healthy purpose-driven small group balances the five purposes of the church.* Most small groups emphasize Bible study, fellowship, and prayer. But God has called us to reach out to others as well. In sessions 4 and 5 you'll have a chance to take small steps in serving others in your group and in making a difference to people outside your group. If the five purposes are new to your group, be sure to review the Read Me First section with your new group. In addition, the Frequently Asked Questions section could help your group understand some of the purpose-driven group basics.

Question 2. An agreement is an opportunity to raise the bar of commitment, even for established groups. When you talk about things like attendance and group ownership, people begin to envision what their group could be like if they lived these values. So turn to page 61 and take five or ten minutes to look at the Purpose-Driven Group Agreement. Read each value aloud in turn, and let group members comment at the end. Emphasize confidentiality—a commitment that is essential to the ability to trust each other.

"Spiritual Health" says that group members give permission to encourage each other to set spiritual goals *for themselves*. As the study progresses, a group member may set a goal to do daily devotions, or a dad may set a goal to spend half an hour each evening with his children. No one will set goals for someone else; each person will be free to set his or her own goals.

Regarding expectations: It's amazing how many groups never take the time to make explicit plans about refreshments, child care, and other such issues. Child care is a big issue in many groups. It's important to treat it as an issue that the group as a whole needs to solve, even if the group decides that each member will make arrangements separately.

If you feel that your group needs to move on, you can save the conversation about expectations until your next meeting.

If new members join your group in future sessions, be sure to share the agreement with them.

Question 3. Have someone read the Bible passage aloud. It's a good idea to ask someone ahead of time, because not everyone is comfortable reading aloud in public. When the passage has been read, ask question 3. It is *not* necessary that everyone answer every question in the Bible study. In fact, a group can become tiresome and boring if you simply go around the circle and give answers. Your goal is to create a discussion—which means that perhaps only a few people respond to each question, and an engaging dialogue gets going.

Question 4. We can love God by talking honestly and intimately with him, by learning more about what he wants done in the world and committing ourselves to doing it, by making him a priority with our time, and so on.

Don't be afraid to allow silence while people think. It's completely normal to have periods of silence in a Bible study. You might count to seven silently. If nobody says anything, say something humorous such as, "I can wait longer than you can!" Remember, too, that it's not necessary for everyone to respond to every one of the Bible study questions.

Question 6. There isn't a stark right or wrong answer to this question. Allow the group to discuss both sides. Some people have an intimate relationship with God but stand aloof from the people around them. In the opening story of this session, Denise talks about how she learned about loving God before she learned how to love a husband. On the other hand, a genuine love for God ought to overflow into love for those whom he loves—which means *everybody.* First John 4:19–21 says, "We love because [God] first loved us. If anyone says, 'I love God,' yet hates his brother, he is a liar. For anyone who does not love his brother, whom he has seen, cannot love God, whom he has not seen. And he has given us this command: Whoever loves God must also love his brother." In this passage, John broadens our understanding of what loving God means so that we see that it includes obeying his instruction to love others. John is highly skeptical of anyone who claims to love the invisible God but can't manage to love a flesh-and-blood person.

Question 8. Jesus carries on his theme of love, but he focuses on a particular group of our neighbors, namely, our fellow Christians. Interestingly, this special attention to relationships with fellow believers has an outward-looking purpose—that outsiders will be drawn into the circle of love when they see the unusual love we have for each other. Love is constantly looking to widen the circle. So now we have three love commands: love God, love our fellow Christians, and love people who are not Christians but are still "neighbors" far and near.

Questions 11-12. The open chair is a vivid symbol of one of the values in the Purpose-Driven Group Agreement—"Inviting People." Some groups fear that newcomers will interrupt the intimacy that members have built over time. However, groups that use the open chair generally gain strength with the infusion of new blood. It's like a river of living water flowing into a stagnant pond. Some groups remain permanently open, while others choose to open periodically, such as at the beginning and ending of a study. Love grows by giving itself away. If your circle becomes too large for easy face-to-face conversations, you can simply form a second discussion circle in another room in your home.

Give people a quiet moment or two in which to write down a name. Then have them share the names. You might pray for these names later in your session. Encourage people not to be afraid to invite others into the group.

Before you leave the meeting, decide who will lead your discussion next week and where you will meet. Rotating leaders and hosts gives everyone a chance to develop their strengths. Encourage whomever will be the leader to read through the leadership sections in preparation for next week's study.

If you have an existing group, some group members may resist structural change—or any kind of change for that matter. Encourage them to test-drive the new format with an open mind, and see what God may do. You never know—it may generate fresh gusts of wind for the sails of your group.

SESSION TWO: CONNECTING WITH GOD'S FAMILY

Goals of this Session

- To explore what's involved in genuinely connecting with others
- To be motivated to attend the rest of the sessions of this group

Especially helpful for this session: Leadership Lifters #5 and #6

New rotating leaders may want to meet ahead of time with an experienced leader to review the plan for the meeting. You may want to have some extra booklets on hand for any new group members.

Question 1. As leader, you should be the first to answer this question. Your answer will model the amount of time and vulnerability you want others to imitate. If you are brief, others will be brief. If your answer is superficial, you'll set a superficial tone—but if you tell something substantive and personal, others will know that your group is a safe place to tell the truth about themselves.

In the Bible study section (GROWING) of your meeting, it's not necessary for everyone to respond to every question. But in the CONNECTING section, everyone should respond unless they prefer to pass.

Question 2. We hope to spend eternity with God and his family. This is a promise about which we don't need to be in doubt. We also hope to be transformed in our bodies as Jesus was transformed after his resurrection (1 Corinthians 15:35–55) and to have our souls transformed to be like him in his character (1 John 3:2–3). We hope for God to say, "Well done, good and faithful servant!" (Matthew 25:21). We also have hopes for this life. We hope to become increasingly like Jesus in our ability to love God and others (2 Corinthians 3:18). We have good reason to hope that we will increasingly be able to respond to life's ups and downs with grace and patience.

Question 5. Meeting together is a laboratory in which we learn to love others. It's also a source of support when positive responses to life are hard for us. If we're on our own it's easy to drift into merely holding beliefs about God. Meeting together helps us live what we believe.

Question 8. It's important to do this exercise in a spirit of grace. Nobody is perfect. These are simply a few examples of what a real connection with others involves. These items are goals for you to pursue as your group continues on in your life together.

The Purpose-Driven Life Health Plan on pages 68–70 is a tool to help people be more focused in setting goals for spiritual health. It contains suggested goals, questions to think about, and a chart for keeping track of feedback from spiritual partners. Point it out and encourage group members to use it if it seems helpful. You may also want to consult your Small Group Calendar (page 63) to see who might lead your discussion next time.

SESSION THREE:
GROWING TO BE LIKE CHRIST

Goals of this Session

- To learn what it means to live in Jesus Christ—not just in theory but in practice
- To take a step toward deepening your life together with God

Especially helpful for this session: Leadership Lifters #8 and #9

Question 1. You could choose a high point of your spiritual life, such as a retreat, or you could choose a painful situation that taught you something. If you are the first to answer, others will get the idea and follow your example.

Question 2. This seems like an obvious question, but some reflection will help the group get the most out of the word picture Jesus is painting. The answer is not simply "the vine." What enables a branch to bear fruit is the nourishment that comes from the soil and goes up through the roots of the vine and into the branch. Ancient farmers couldn't explain all the science, but they knew that the vine was somehow a source of life and nourishment for the branches.

In English it's awkward to speak of a branch *living in* a vine. We might speak of being connected to the vine. *Living in* means "drawing life from."

Question 4. Making a home in Jesus certainly begins with trusting him as our Savior and believing what the Bible says about him. But as the study notes on page 35 suggest, believing in him without acting daily on those beliefs makes no sense. To live in him involves doing what he says. The catch is that we're often unable by means of sheer willpower to do what he says. "Love one another," he says, but we often find love difficult. That's why making a home in Jesus necessarily leads us to make choices that enable us to draw nourishment from him. We need to make choices about how we use our time and our minds. We need to devote chunks of quality time to being with God—both alone and with others. We need to devote time to taking in what he has said to us in the Bible and to receiving the nourishment that comes as we pray and worship. We also need to develop the habit of thinking about God as we go through our day. This is often called "practicing the presence of God." We need to bring the reality of God before our minds routinely so that this reality nourishes our thoughts, feelings, and actions.

Certainly we are saved by grace through faith alone, not because we love well or pray every day. But if saving faith doesn't lead to actions such as praying and loving, then we may have our tickets to heaven but our lives here on earth will not delight God's heart.

Question 6. Galatians 5:22–23 offers one portrait of a fruitful Christian—a person who thinks and acts with love, joy, peace, patience, kindness, goodness, faithfulness, gentleness, and self-control. We are also fruitful when we foster Jesus' life in another person's life—when we draw someone else to greater love or to new faith, for example.

Question 8. Jesus isn't interested in making us feel bad; he's interested in motivating us to live differently. This means making space in our lives for him. You can acknowledge that it's profoundly challenging to make time in our busy lives to become quiet and draw nourishment from Jesus Christ. But we simply *must* make hard decisions about our priorities in order to carve out time for this crucial relationship.

Question 9. People are much more likely to follow through with their commitment to spend daily time with God if they have the support of a friend. Read Leadership Lifters #8 and #9 on pages 82–83. Why not have group members identify spiritual partners right now? Point out the Spiritual Partners' Check-In Page on page 71, which can give partners a structure for checking in with each other. Also remind group members of the sample journal page on page 103.

Question 11. This exercise is simply a time-honored method of meditating on the Bible (Psalm 1:2, 119:15). It's quite different from Buddhist meditation, because its goal is to fill your mind with the words of God. It will help you take in God's words at a deeper level. As the leader, you should keep track of the time. To some, two minutes of silence will feel like a lot.

Goals of this Session

- To realize that God has entrusted you with his work and his resources
- To decide how you can use your unique design for service in your group

Especially helpful for this session: Leadership Lifter #7

Question 3. The third servant believed that the master used his own resources to further expand his resources (which was true) and that this business skill made him a "hard man" (which was the servant's interpretation). He interpreted the master's expectations, not as an invitation to creativity, but as demands, even threats. He was scared of his master and focused on his master's inclination to punish folly. By contrast, we can infer that the other two servants knew equally well the master's attitude toward resources but interpreted his character differently. Perhaps they saw his wisdom and his delight in the creative use of resources for good.

Question 4. In order to be investors rather than hoarders, we need to believe that we have resources and that we are capable of investing them wisely. We need some confidence. We also need to believe that learning to invest wisely is worth our time.

Question 6. Among other things, God has entrusted each group member with material goods, skills, lessons learned through experience, natural abilities, spiritual gifts, and a personality that has particular strengths.

Question 7. Think ahead of time about your own challenges. Fear might be one. Others could be busyness, a belief that other things are more important, lack of training, and lack of support.

Question 9. People are often reluctant to volunteer to do something in the group for fear that others will think they are prideful or unequipped for the task. They are more willing to take a step of service when they feel the group affirming their abilities. This exercise is a chance to help all group members take ownership of the group—moving from being the leader's group to being *our* group. The leader doesn't cease to shepherd the group, but he or she no longer has to shoulder all the weight. You may not need help running your group, but your group members need opportunities to serve. Small steps within the group will lead to larger steps of service outside the group. Your job is to help each group member develop into an effective servant. Doing so includes allowing others to experiment with leading a prayer time or a Bible study. You are "[preparing] God's people for works of service, so that the body of Christ may be built up" (Ephesians 4:12). Try to think of one thing each group member has to offer. Your affirmation will mean a great deal.

Ask group members to take a moment on their own to review the list of service opportunities and check one or two areas they'd like to be involved in. If no one volunteers for an area, let the group say who they think would be good in that area. Ask people to go beyond what they love to do and consider what they *can* do to build up the group. Encourage group members to think of additional ideas they'd like to see become a reality in the group.

Even if people aren't ready to volunteer for responsibilities yet, use this time to affirm one another. Sometimes it's a blessing to have the group give words of affirmation to each member. This is an opportunity to help your group draw closer together.

Before you leave the meeting, decide who will lead your discussion next week and where you will meet. Rotating leaders and hosts gives everyone a chance to develop their strengths.

Goals of this Session

- To explore how you can be light in a dark world
- To begin to make sharing Jesus Christ part of your life together by praying for non-Christians you know

Especially helpful for this session: Leadership Lifters #2 and #5

Question 2. Light represents God, goodness, and truth. You are the presence of God in the world. Others should be able to look at your life and see what God is like. They should see the reality of his goodness, wisdom, love, graciousness, generosity, justice, and other qualities.

Question 3. In Matthew 6, Jesus explains what he *doesn't* mean by the good deeds that outsiders will see. In verse 1 Jesus says, "Be careful not to do your 'acts of righteousness' before men, to be seen by them." So what are the "good deeds" we are supposed to let the world see, and what are the "acts of righteousness" we should keep private? The "acts of righteousness" are spiritual practices such as prayer, fasting, and giving to the poor (Matthew 6:1–18). Practices like these are intended for us—to help us grow spiritually. They don't impress unbelievers (in fact, unbelievers can be put off if we seem overly "religious"). These practices often do impress other believers, so Jesus warns us that if we show off in front of fellow believers in this way, we are likely to drain these practices of their spiritual value. The "good deeds" that draw unbelievers to faith are demonstrations of character; they are acts that show courage, kindness, generosity, and love. Remaining tenderhearted and brave when we face a challenge is an example. Another example is treating a mean person with kindness. Honesty at work can demonstrate our light to the world, especially in a workplace where cutting corners is common.

Encourage group members to be as specific as possible about the good deeds they can do (or are doing) to display God's light.

Question 5. Light-bearing behavior emerges from those who take time to reflect on their own sins, to forgive others who hurt them, to notice people's needs, and to fill their minds with the goodness of God. The point of Bible reading is to fill your mind with God's goodness. Read and reflect on how Jesus behaved. Pay attention to how you behave, and be ready to confess sin when necessary. Allow your heart to be moved by others. It's also helpful to have a few close friends with whom you can discuss these things.

Question 6. Our light dims when we're too busy and stressed to fill our minds with God, to notice others, or to reflect on how we're acting. It's hard to be gracious when we're rushed. For many of us, the decision to cut back on activity is the most important step we can take.

Question 7. Non-Christians will take notice when they see that you relate to people in a significantly different way from the way most people relate. Your family or group can be light by inviting outsiders into your midst and living life together in front of them. Make friends with non-Christians. Welcome them into your home. Take your whole family or group to do a service project. Have a party as a group, and invite non-Christians to join you. Don't worry about letting them see your imperfect kids; let them see the gracious way you deal with imperfect kids. And if your grace-filled parenting skills are a little weak, maybe having unbelievers around will motivate you to seek God's help in that area!

Question 9. Praying for people is a great way to cultivate care for them. As you pray for them, you'll begin to see needs in their lives that the gospel addresses. Also, prayer actually affects things on a spiritual level. It's a profoundly crucial part of God's work to soften someone's heart. Give people about a minute to write a name down. Almost everyone knows at least one non-Christian! Then gather a name from each person to form the group's Top Ten list.

Question 10. This question is theoretical—"what if" your group had a party. But it's actually not hard to have such a party. Your model is Matthew 9:9–12. Who in your group would be willing to host a party for seekers? Whom will you invite?

Some groups make such parties a regular part of their life together. They meet three times a month with group members only, and in the fourth week they have a social gathering for their friends who don't know Jesus.

SESSION SIX:
SURRENDERING YOUR LIFE
FOR GOD'S PLEASURE

Goals of this Session

- To reflect on what it means to surrender your whole lives to God
- To celebrate the end of this study by affirming what each group member offers

Especially helpful for this session: Leadership Lifters #10

Question 1. People have very different reactions to the word *surrender*. This question aims to get these reactions on the table so they're not lurking at the back of people's minds. For some, *surrender* has overtones of feminine sexuality—and this isn't necessarily very appealing to men. Some people think *surrender* sounds passive, like "giving up." Nothing could be further from the truth—*surrender* is as manly and active as trusting the judgment of a commanding officer. It's a shift from resisting God's authority to accepting God's authority. It's not entirely passive at all; we must *actively* trust and obey God. It's an act of confidence and hope, not a despairing kind of "giving up." But it does take humility, and that's where most of us struggle.

Question 2. Weeping over one's sin often serves as a prelude to worship. The woman poured out a costly possession to demonstrate her tremendous love for the one who forgave her sins. Kissing someone's feet and pouring expensive perfume on them is adoration either of a sexual or a spiritual kind. This woman humbled herself about as low as she could go and treated Jesus as having supreme value. This is what worship involves—making ourselves small and God big in our eyes. Our society emphasizes self-esteem, so we tend to despise groveling. But this woman groveled to a shocking degree. And Jesus treated her as though her groveling didn't humiliate her but actually conferred honor on her. It's a paradox: Lowering ourselves before God's majesty is the route to true exaltation; puffing ourselves up only ends up diminishing us.

Question 3. In Jesus' day, people showed a deep concern for honor and shame. Being honored by a shameful person (someone we would call "a loser") made you a loser, too. Simon thought the woman was scum, so he thought any honor from her was worse than worthless. Jesus, of course, did not think the woman was scum. Simon also judged her behavior to be disgraceful—as it surely would have been if the object of her adoration had been anyone but Jesus.

Question 6. The chief purpose of church worship services is to lavish this kind of passionate love on Jesus. The chief purpose of *private* thanksgiving and praise to God is to do the same. Finally, our every act of surrender and obedience—our every act of loving another human being—is an act of love toward Jesus Christ (Matthew 25:37–40).

Question 8. Be sure to reserve ten minutes to review your Purpose-Driven Group Agreement. The end of a study is a chance to evaluate what has been good and what could be improved on in your group. It's a time for some people to bow out gracefully and for others to recommit for a new season. If you're planning to go on to another study in the DOING LIFE TOGETHER series, session 1 of that study will reintroduce the agreement. You don't have to discuss it again then if you do so now.

Question 9. The reason we suggest you do this exercise in pairs is that some people may want to surrender issues they won't talk about in front of the whole group. One man with another man (or one woman with another woman) may be willing to be more candid. However, if you're confident of your group's intimacy, then feel free to do this exercise as a whole group. It's important that no one feel pressured to surrender something specific.

You may want to close your meeting with a time of worship, such as singing a song, reading a psalm together, or worshiping silently with a song from a CD. Session 4 invited group members to contribute to a worship experience in session 6. If the time is right for this, check in with people ahead of time to verify your plans.

You may also want to celebrate the end of this study in some way. You can share a meal, enjoy refreshments together, go out for dessert, or plan a party for your next meeting. Your group may be coming to an end, or you may be planning to continue—whatever the case, it's good to celebrate when you finish something.

ABOUT THE AUTHORS

Brett and Dee Eastman have served at Saddleback Valley Community Church since July 1997, after previously serving for five years at Willow Creek Community Church in Illinois. Brett's primary responsibilities are in the areas of small groups, strategic planning, and leadership development. Brett has earned his Masters of Divinity degree from Talbot School of Theology and his Management Certificate from Kellogg School of Business at Northwestern University. Dee is the real hero in the family, who, after giving birth to Joshua and Breanna, gave birth to identical triplets—Meagan, Melody, and Michelle. Dee is the coleader of the women's Bible study at Saddleback Church called "The Journey." They live in Las Flores, California.

Todd and Denise Wendorff have served at Saddleback Valley Community Church since 1998. Todd is a pastor in the Maturity Department at Saddleback, and Denise coleads a women's Bible class with Dee Eastman called "The Journey." Todd earned a Masters of Theology degree from Talbot School of Theology. He has taught Biblical Studies courses at Biola University, Golden Gate Seminary, and other universities. Previously, Todd and Denise served at Willow Creek Community Church. They love to help others learn to dig into God's Word for themselves and experience biblical truths in their lives. Todd and Denise live in Trabuco Canyon, California, with their three children, Brooke, Brittany, and Brandon.

Karen Lee-Thorp has written or cowritten more than fifty books, workbooks, and Bible studies. Her books include *A Compact Guide to the Christian Life*, *How to Ask Great Questions*, and *Why Beauty Matters*. She was a senior editor at NavPress for many years and series editor for the LifeChange Bible study series. She is now a freelance writer living in Brea, California, with her husband, Greg Herr, and their daughters, Megan and Marissa.

SMALL GROUP ROSTER

Name	Address	Phone	E-mail Address	Team or Role	Church Ministry
Bill Jones	7 Alvalar Street L.F. 92665	766-2255	bjones@aol.com	Socials	children's ministry

Be sure to pass your booklets around the room the first night, or have someone volunteer to type the group roster for all members. Encourage group ownership by having each member share a team role or responsibility.

Name	Address	Phone	E-mail Address	Team or Role	Church Ministry

Today's Passage: _____

Reflections from my HEART:

I *Honor* who you are. (Praise God for something.)

I *Express* who I'm not. (Confess any known sin.)

I *Affirm* who I am in you. (How does God see you?)

I *Request* your will for me. (Ask God for something.)

I *Thank* you for what you've done. (Thank him for something.)

Today's Action Step:

The Purpose-Driven® Life
WHAT ON EARTH AM I HERE FOR?

RICK WARREN

The most basic question everyone faces in life is *Why am I here? What is my purpose?* Self-help books suggest that people should look within, at their own desires and dreams, but Rick Warren says the starting place must be with God—and his eternal purposes for each life. Real meaning and significance comes from understanding and fulfilling God's purposes for putting us on earth.

The Purpose-Driven Life takes the groundbreaking message of the award-winning *Purpose-Driven Church* and goes deeper, applying it to the lifestyle of individual Christians. This book helps readers understand God's incredible plan for their lives. Warren enables them to see "the big picture" of what life is all about and begin to live the life God created them to live.

The Purpose-Driven Life is a manifesto for Christian living in the 21st century—a lifestyle based on eternal purposes, not cultural values. Using biblical stories and letting the Bible speak for itself, Warren clearly explains God's 5 purposes for each of us:

We were planned for God's pleasure—experience real worship.
We were formed for God's family—enjoy real fellowship.
We were created to become like Christ —learn real discipleship.
We were shaped for serving God—practice real ministry.
We were made for a mission —live out real evangelism.

This long-anticipated book is the life-message of Rick Warren, founding pastor of Saddleback Church. Written in a captivating devotional style, the book is divided into 40 short chapters that can be read as a daily devotional, studied by small groups, and used by churches participating in the nationwide "40 Days of Purpose" campaign.

Hardcover: 0-310-20571-9   Unabridged Audio Pages® CD: 0-310-24788-8
Unabridged Audio Pages® cassette: 0-310-20907-2

Also available from Inspirio, the gift division of Zondervan

Purpose-Driven Life Journal:	0-310-80306-3
Planned for God's Pleasure (Gift Book):	0-310-80322-5
ScriptureKeeper® Plus Purpose-Driven® Life:	0-310-80323-3

CONNECTING WITH GOD'S FAMILY

BRETT AND DEE EASTMAN;
TODD AND DENISE WENDORFF;
KAREN LEE-THORP

God longs for you to have rich, genuine connections with him and a handful of other people. These six sessions will help you connect more deeply with Jesus Christ and build genuine relationships with Christian friends. Christ's love makes it possible for you to be known and to know others, to be loved and to love, to resolve conflict effectively, and to move outward together in faith.

> "Doing Life Together is a groundbreaking study . . . [It's] the first small group curriculum built completely on the purpose-driven paradigm . . . The greatest reason I'm excited about it is that I've seen the dramatic changes [it] produces in the lives of those who study it."
>
> —FROM THE FOREWORD BY RICK WARREN

Based on the five biblical purposes that form the bedrock of Saddleback Church, Doing Life Together is a comprehensive study of the Purpose-Driven Life. It will help you cultivate a healthy, balanced Christian life together with a friend, small group, or even your entire church. This experienced team of writers will take you on a spiritual journey, discovering not only what God created you for but how you can turn that dream into an everyday reality. Experience the transformation firsthand as you begin Connecting, Growing, Developing, Sharing, and Surrendering your life together for him.

Softcover ISBN: 0-310-24673-3

Pick up a copy today at your favorite bookstore!

ZONDERVAN™

GRAND RAPIDS, MICHIGAN 49530 USA

WWW.ZONDERVAN.COM

GROWING TO BE LIKE CHRIST

BRETT AND DEE EASTMAN;
TODD AND DENISE WENDORFF;
KAREN LEE-THORP

Spiritual maturity doesn't happen by accident. The six sessions in this study equip you for the basic habits of spiritual growth: relying on the Holy Spirit, cultivating time in the Bible and prayer, seeing life's obstacles as opportunities for growth, and partnering with Christians who are committed to supporting your growth. Here is a realistic, practical path to growing strong in faith and Christian character.

"Doing Life Together is a groundbreaking study . . . [It's] the first small group curriculum built completely on the purpose-driven paradigm . . . The greatest reason I'm excited about it is that I've seen the dramatic changes [it] produces in the lives of those who study it."
—FROM THE FOREWORD BY RICK WARREN

Based on the five biblical purposes that form the bedrock of Saddleback Church, Doing Life Together is a comprehensive study of the Purpose-Driven Life. It will help you cultivate a healthy, balanced Christian life together with a friend, small group, or even your entire church. This experienced team of writers will take you on a spiritual journey, discovering not only what God created you for but how you can turn that dream into an everyday reality. Experience the transformation firsthand as you begin Connecting, Growing, Developing, Sharing, and Surrendering your life together for him.

Softcover ISBN: 0-310-24674-1

Pick up a copy today at your favorite bookstore!

ZONDERVAN™

GRAND RAPIDS, MICHIGAN 49530 USA
WWW.ZONDERVAN.COM

DEVELOPING YOUR SHAPE TO SERVE OTHERS

BRETT AND DEE EASTMAN;
TODD AND DENISE WENDORFF;
KAREN LEE-THORP

The way you're wired is no accident! God designed your unique mix of gifts, natural abilities, personality, values, and life experiences to play an essential part in his kingdom. These six sessions will help you develop your God-given design at home, at work, at church, and in your community in a way that extends God's love to others and enriches your own life immeasurably.

"Doing Life Together is a groundbreaking study ... [It's] the first small group curriculum built completely on the purpose-driven paradigm ... The greatest reason I'm excited about it is that I've seen the dramatic changes [it] produces in the lives of those who study it."

–FROM THE FOREWORD BY RICK WARREN

Based on the five biblical purposes that form the bedrock of Saddleback Church, Doing Life Together is a comprehensive study of the Purpose-Driven Life. It will help you cultivate a healthy, balanced Christian life together with a friend, small group, or even your entire church. This experienced team of writers will take you on a spiritual journey, discovering not only what God created you for but how you can turn that dream into an everyday reality. Experience the transformation firsthand as you begin Connecting, Growing, Developing, Sharing, and Surrendering your life together for him.

Softcover ISBN: 0-310-24675-X

Pick up a copy today at your favorite bookstore!

ZONDERVAN™

GRAND RAPIDS, MICHIGAN 49530 USA
WWW.ZONDERVAN.COM

SHARING YOUR
LIFE MISSION EVERY DAY

Brett and Dee Eastman;
Todd and Denise Wendorff;
Karen Lee-Thorp

Sharing Your Life Mission Every Day just isn't that hard. You need a few skills, a few friends for support, and a glimpse of God's heart for those who don't know him. These six sessions will equip you to extend love to seekers around you and talk about your experience with God in ways that people will understand. God doesn't ask you to do it alone—discover the power that comes from teaming up!

"Doing Life Together is a groundbreaking study ... [It's] the first small group curriculum built completely on the purpose-driven paradigm ... The greatest reason I'm excited about it is that I've seen the dramatic changes [it] produces in the lives of those who study it."

–FROM THE FOREWORD BY RICK WARREN

Based on the five biblical purposes that form the bedrock of Saddleback Church, Doing Life Together is a comprehensive study of the Purpose-Driven Life. It will help you cultivate a healthy, balanced Christian life together with a friend, small group, or even your entire church. This experienced team of writers will take you on a spiritual journey, discovering not only what God created you for but how you can turn that dream into an everyday reality. Experience the transformation firsthand as you begin Connecting, Growing, Developing, Sharing, and Surrendering your life together for him.

Softcover ISBN: 0-310-24676-8

Pick up a copy today at your favorite bookstore!

GRAND RAPIDS, MICHIGAN 49530 USA

WWW.ZONDERVAN.COM

SURRENDERING YOUR LIFE FOR GOD'S PLEASURE

BRETT AND DEE EASTMAN;
TODD AND DENISE WENDORFF;
KAREN LEE-THORP

What does it mean to surrender to God? These six sessions will help you experience the transforming power of a surrendered life. As you learn to worship Jesus Christ throughout your daily life, you will come to trust him with the experiences of your past, the precious things of your present, and your hopes for the future. What are you holding on to? Discover the peace of laying it at God's feet.

> "Doing Life Together is a groundbreaking study . . . [It's] the first small group curriculum built completely on the purpose-driven paradigm . . . The greatest reason I'm excited about it is that I've seen the dramatic changes [it] produces in the lives of those who study it."
>
> –FROM THE FOREWORD BY RICK WARREN

Based on the five biblical purposes that form the bedrock of Saddleback Church, Doing Life Together is a comprehensive study of the Purpose-Driven Life. It will help you cultivate a healthy, balanced Christian life together with a friend, small group, or even your entire church. This experienced team of writers will take you on a spiritual journey, discovering not only what God created you for but how you can turn that dream into an everyday reality. Experience the transformation firsthand as you begin Connecting, Growing, Developing, Sharing, and Surrendering your life together for him.

Softcover ISBN: 0-310-24677-6

Pick up a copy today at your favorite bookstore!

ZONDERVAN™

GRAND RAPIDS, MICHIGAN 49530 USA

WWW.ZONDERVAN.COM